UNAPOLOGETIC

Johnny Francis Wolf

author of
MEN UNLIKE OTHERS

A Wild Ink Publishing Original
Wild Ink Publishing
wild-ink-publishing.com

Copyright © 2023 by Johnny Francis Wolf

ISBN: (Hardcover) 978-1-958531-47-1
ISBN: (Paperback) 978-1-958531-48-8

I've always related, in a spirit animal way, to the canine. Hyena to Werewolf. Complete with all their lore.

My life changed perspective, was released from its cage, when I first read Hesse. I longed to be the wolf of the Steppes... and began to cultivate the same. To live it.

My point? We've all seen and lived this before. Different archetypes. Vampires, the monsters under the bed... truth is, the call is coming from inside the house.

This is about Johnny. Based on my experience with his words. Hesse-like, survivalist, street, sexual, and all the things needed on a trip to *today*.

They make me know him.

I see myself, likewise, surviving and clawing my way towards a domestication of sorts. Polishing both the human and beast, goading them through their necessary and constant morphing.

An educated survivalist. He waves pen and story.

His book is a fine example of that. You will walk away with a friend, you will be stronger. You will live life, as it comes, more easily.

Lives change. Books like this facilitate that.

No blurbs or sales pitch. Dig in wise ones... feel the pages. Run your fingers along the black text. Breathe a little. Bleed a little.

Jack Varnell
author - artist - creative - podcaster - friend
socialyetdistanced.com
allmylinks.com/jackvarnell

Dedication

Some years ago, when living in New Mexico, Christmas arrived with me, my roommate, her son.. all broke.

Barely two nickels to rub together between the lot of us, gifts would have to wait that year.

"Instead.. write Carl and I, each, a poem," Rhonda suggested. *"I've always loved your playing with verse,"* she added.

I did.

—

I had not dabbled much in writing, prior. Poetry, couplets, rhyming were ever gambles I'd hazard a stab.. but only now and again.

I was, howbeit, that Holiday Season, in the midst of penning (attempting to pen) a script.

An actor not working, I thought I could fashion my own vehicle, a role in a film I would scribe (much as Billy Bob Thornton did for himself with SLING BLADE). Pipe dream, no doubt (and a screenplay that was never optioned), it was a venture that appealed to me..

challenging my unlettered writing skills.

Not schooled in the fundamentals of photoplay, I reasoned poetry, photos, song links might be nice sprinkled throughout the dialogue and action. I had no one telling me different.

Rhonda found all this fun.

I recall her sitting on the side of my bed, suffering through my emotive enactments..

the script pages I wrote that day.

"I think I like the poems best," she'd often opine at the end of my overwrought readings.

—

So.. I blame (thank) Rhonda Lynne Wingo for this book.

Though none of these tales are derived from said screenplay (nor much from that penniless Christmas made mention), they reflect her advisement that following New Year's Eve..

"Maybe you should start a Facebook Page for your poetry.. drafting one per day..   at least for a year."

—

When too cold to wear
ONE'S HEART on one's sleeve..

With all that we STRIVE FOR
sans hope to achieve...

Open your eyes,
maybe SQUINT to perceive.

The choice is TO GIVE.
In love we receive.

— excerpt from ***EVE***
(my inelegant gift to Rhonda that lean Noël)

Introduction

I can't recall her exact words. It was the first review conferred upon my new Daily Poem Fan Page. The reviewer and I were, yet, official Facebook friends.

"I would like to sit beneath a tree.. alone in a grove, sipping a cool drink. I crack the book's spine, flip through its pages. My head finds a soft place, leaning against the tree's yielding bark.. the blanket beneath me, plaid and fuzzy. I spend my afternoon reading Johnny's verse.."

or something quite similar. A poet as well, it would surprise no one familiar with her style were the exact words even more balmy than those my memory managed to summon up.

Ayo Gutierrez thusly first reached out.

Seems most of the reviews on my Page have fallen victim to Facebook's many subsequent schematic revisions (with Ayo's appraisal, sadly, one of the missing). But the impression it made was lasting. It's never too far from my heart when I raise a quill or tap on a keyboard.

—

And write, I did, daily and more. A dribble, a deluge, depending the day.

The online sharing was everything, the comments from friends were kinder than I deserved, the encouragement enlivening.

I would not be a writer today had I not braved the internet criticism (received plenty) and risked the potential online plagiarism (though I've always held such social media word thieves could find better bards to steal from).. had I not sought out an audience to tender my tales.

I am forever indebted to the mentors I met, the friendships I forged, the learning-by-reading the brilliant words they, too, shared on Facebook.

—

Mine are bald and artless yarns with thorny roots and frizzy leaves. Some feel unfinished. All remain unpolished.

I'm nervous revisiting this simpler time, rereading the runes of someone more dewy-eyed.. inking, as I did then, with impulsive and unguarded ease.

Unapologetic, seems.

Left to my own devices, I might hide these prequel iterations.

The resulting primordial ooze now sits before you.. a gathering of raw, awkward phrases and sing-songy rhymes that dare the reader to look past the grammar (or lack thereof) and find the bold, unripened core, the pits, the pith..

the skin unpeeled.

—

Now Ayo, my first mentor.. an esteemed author, teacher, and acclaimed publisher in her own right.. has her book.

"Can I find you a tree, offer a cool drink, dear friend? I may have a blanket to lend.."

Amor

Beasts

Colors

Ego

Family

Pearly Gates

Tender Years

Writing

Amor

age less

I think it never fades for us
in chrysalis, we stay the fuss

    fast the feeling, fervor, fond
    yet to find a magic wand

break the ache that needs for touch
wrinkles gather inasmuch

    as heretofore they line our eyes
    quotation marks for neath, what lies

under reigns a younger soul
who sees themself a modest goal

    for someone else's kindred whim
    someone looking, drawn to him

or her or them or furry friend
need their touch to rise, ascend

    heavy foot on felling worth
    seeking love seems lift from earth

Back

(at Fran)

You look to see if
I am here. And yet I move
again —

      another place, I turn, and then

I spy you
track in slower
time, forgetting rhyme —

with newly rippled, rhythmic
crush of circles,
swelling
torso, telling.

Wetter now,
deep in
mud

there beneath your feet.

      Higher, eyes to lips we meet.

: :

I wade out in the shallow end where waves
eat wrinkles in our toes.

Standing now, am almost froze.

Please look back —

You do, I think

— as see me looking back. I sink.

Still worried, as you worry too,
that you and I have not
yet drowned,

     remain, we hope, as two unfound.

Or even
further, not yet
walked the sand or swam.
In reeds,

I am.

              : :

To distant shore where towels wait to dry
the drops that fortify,
that weigh us,
burn, as will
us turn.

Fretting, always betting, yet —
hoping you stay
likewise

wet.

Promise
ever — I will too,

     and looking forward, back at you.

dictionary

WRITE WHAT YOU KNOW.. so then I know PAIN
for much of my verse is heavy with hurt

SING ME A SONG as whittle my name
carve it in stone half-buried in dirt

:   :

WRITE WHAT YOU KNOW.. so then I know SWEET
with poems I've penned dreaming of love

SING ME A SONG, I pray that we meet
pinning our clouds to welkin above

:   :

WRITE WHAT YOU KNOW.. so then I know FUN
all silly and dumb, ridiculous things

SING ME A SONG of midnight and sun
goading me giggle as wagging my wings

:   :

WRITE WHAT YOU KNOW.. so then I know SEX
as seem to be drawn to anyone nude

SING ME A SONG and tell me you're next
this kind of hunger is less about food

:   :

WRITE WHAT YOU KNOW.. so then I know LOSS
if losing my mind and finding no words

SING ME A SONG to tally the cost
read me my rhymes and tell me I'm heard

ERASER

Picture sunlight blazing BLACK,
   CHALK beneath on wooden track.

In the air, swirls of DUSTY
   FELTED powder, old-school musty.

Maybe LIFE could be like that,
   etch your LOVER 'pon the matte.

FERVOR found be counterfeit?
   Grab the brick, erase the TWIT.

free lunch

    placard with a blocky font
beckoned, bid me eat

    feasting not my normal wont
spending thus, effete

    way to keep one's waist in check
lack of food the prime

    example of a diet, heck
method.. lack of dime

    leave your wallet at the door
leave your pockets bare

    leave your coins in what you wore
yesterday, I swear

    never will you tempted be
buy a sandwich, fries

    thinner, ever, look at me
gaunt beneath my eyes

    same applies to craving love
I've mastered this, an art

    leave behind, in box do shove
all semblance of a heart

HALLMARK CARD

Fairer Maiden, they could try
conjure up with Artist's eye.

      Pen and paint would sing off key,
      never touch what Beauty be.

Poets failed since Verse begun,
hair adorned by jealous Sun.

      Skin that shames all silken weaves,
      ageless Splendor never leaves.

Eyes which pierce with wanton reach,
Angel lashes gaze, beseech.

      Lips that bleed their Honeyed drips,
      milky breasts to beckon sips.

Arms and legs that wrap within,
Hips which beg you, journey in.

      Evermore, throughout one's Life,
      none as lovely as your Wife.

Harp of Trees

(painting by Daniel Sherrin)

I yet remember 4 o'clock,
    an afternoon for taking stock.

Leapt with friend along a bank,
    the year escapeth, drawing blank.

But all my words, recall them well,
    with abbey pealing, distant knell..

"Evermore our friendship be
    this simple truth 'tween you and me.

Passion of a grand design
    where loyalty and love combine."

Universe didst pause, it seems,
    quelling prayers and quashing dreams.

Stillness muted silent skies
    'til he, with dry, unblinking eyes..

"Akin to you, I feel a bond,
    but unlike yours, I'm far less fond."

There it was, the plainest fact
    of no accord or lovers' pact.

Strings of heart unplucked by lance,
    with falling trees.. no harp, no dance.

Honeymoon

(between)

Groom wore dusk,
   his bride, blue heaven.
      Shadow dappled, sunlit spun.

Road they ran
   arose as leaven..
      Living tandem, walked as one.

Sky and dirt,
   horizon ending.
      Edge of purlieu where they met.

Ever touching,
   nearly blending..
      Sun first clambers, sinks to set.

Bounded by
   the ocean swells.
      Waves consume their failing path.

Hand in hand
   amongst the shells..
      Together baptized, moonlit bath.

I know this

Saw in her eyes
  as gazed at his skin,

something like love
  about to begin.

Thought I could feel
  the magic she felt,

all that she longed for,
  cards she was dealt.

Nothing he'd want,
  of this I was sure,

nothing he'd need,
  no treatment or cure.

Poem of words
  true by degree,

not about her if
  all about me.

left

eliminate the
underlie

that swims beneath
the sea

remove the myths that
froth and fly

and waves that crash Capri

staying only
aqua blue

nothing but the
still

leaving me to float
with you

and frolic there until

love poem

how much love.. I'll try compose

love you more than hating foes
    love you more than Shakespeare's rose
        love you more than rhyme-less prose
            love you more than words suppose

love you more than sunlight glows
    love you more than hugs enclose
        love you more than Avon flows
            love you more than Heaven knows

love you more than Life I've chose
    love you more than aging slows
        love you more than raree shows
            love you more than loving grows

wakened spooning.. minus clothes

musings of an artist

(painting female nude)

she begged for my attention
    pose was tight as craving touch

pled for lewd invention
    aroused my state observing such

I could not turn away my eyes
    naked black, she beckoned back

thousand soldiers' battle cries
    pressed me launch a bold attack

palette's dream of making love
    blotch and blended battle shared

people, places, stories of
    she and I aquiver there

her behest, I too must strip
    words then whisper, all but hushed

"kiss me, here, my painted lips
    as let me sup your swollen brush"

peut etre

(writing of a woman reading)

black and white and faded gray
lost within a book

model poses, pay to play
posturing a look

gingham plaid and cotton gloves
hair is combed and flipped

pages beckon other loves
eyes are double-dipped

other lives and other lips
a mannequin with soul

tiny waist and shapely hips
seem take on many roles

but something in her far off gaze
is closer, nearer, nigh

penning words that sing her praise
a poet getting high

and still I think she looks at me
reads the words I write

thinking thoughts the camera sees
her staying here tonight

remember climbing Notre-Dame

Her bucket list.. a Paris trip.
    Susan Wolf in cancer's grip.

Queried if I'd like to go..
    my answer quick. It wasn't *no*.

Ile Saint-Louis, tiny bed..
    big, our yen for cheese and bread.

Wine, baguette with smear of brie,
    never-ending.. missing she.

Recall our straying by the Seine..
    feels like saying *bye* again.

River carries Susan's soul,
    and in my heart, a twilight stroll.

Arrondissements of Paris.. sky
    with angels trilling French on high.

Took her name to be my own.
    When call me *Wolf*.. am not alone.

she

(of bookshop)

Surprised, her face inquired why
I called her by her given name.

No *'honey'*, *'dear'* or *'sugar pie'*.
The love I lost I sought reclaim....

"I'm Emily.. and you are... Tom,"
in flashback when we met.

Me, a clerk with nametag on,
"I've not the pleasure yet."

::

Raised my gaze, no more could speak,
'Emily...' I mooned inside.

Awaited her return all week,
my life on hold, tongue still tied.

Towered tomes I hid behind,
her standing there outside the door.

Tall the stack and fate unkind
when knocked the bevy to the floor.

::

And as they tumbled, quite the din,
with me as pink as pig.

As if on cue, she waltzed right in,
buried 'neath I rise, un-dig.

Thus, released of all my fears
(it couldn't get much worse),

we reassembled all the tiers
and laughed, composing verse....

: :

*"There once was student named Tom
whose swagger was quite like a bomb.*

*Books, by the load,
would surely explode.*

An avalanche followed by calm."

: :

And so began a college fling,
two writers living words.

Years of love then wedding rings
as glasses-wearing nerds.

But green, my envy, colored all,
her poems like her name.

Lovely sonnets, mine like scrawl.
She wrote her way to fame.

: :

I got a job, earned a wage,
our marriage by the book.

Lost my pen, was blank my page,
no plot or clever hook.

And there we lay for countless years,
a poet and her spouse.

Polite and caring, dry my tears,
home was but a house.

: :

This morning as I filled my bowl
with Cheerios and spoon,

a thought occurred, released my soul,
our verses out of tune.

Dropped the dish and spilled the cup,
crying out her name....

I pray she helps me pick them up
like years ago, our bookshop game.

SMEAR

The rain washed way the
CHALK REMAINING.

Ever RAINING..

sidewalk artist watches most
from underneath the NEW YORK POST,
tented well in Boy Scout fashion.

Paper soonly wet and dank,
HEAVY LADEN, leaden,
left at feet.

Sodden SHEET...

                    : :

what once was PARIS,
GOLDEN STREET, with lovers
talking, seated, walking up and down
the belle rue.

Remember YOU..

Boy and Girl, hand in hand,
an AUTUMN DAY with awnings striped,

flapping, filled with billows
blowing.

Lips as OWING...

                    : :

falling leaves that eddy heady,
whirling 'bout a LOVE THAT TRIES to
make you think you're
YOUNG.

Me and you who lived AMONG..

small cafés that smelled of MORNING,
outside tables, warm croissants,
clouds above.

With little WARNING...

::

mixing with the NEW YORK rain
as artist, POET feel the same.

Both will cry enough to
help the chalk
to MELT

is
FELT..

Tango

Writhing limbs that twist and flex,
        throbbing beat, percussive sex.

Lacquered tonic glistens hair,
        dapper suit, dress barely there.

Knees together, clinging hips,
        partner's heart and yours eclipse.

Music ends. Real life begins
        bereft of passion, beggared sins..

Play another Tango, please,
        Conga, Cha Cha only tease

as solely Argentine will do.
        Dip me dear, I sin with you.

two

(hiding hind the nice)

her humble neath the fragile soft

as pale beyond the black

his lips and eyes and thorns aloft

are launched by hidden lack

V-J Day

(1945)

Screaming Headline, black & white..

    "JAPAN SURRENDERS!" End of fight.

Sailor catching Nurse in flight...

    Times Square kiss. Hot August night.

wet street

Season when the asphalt shines,
a river running through.

Steady rain and storylines,
night is dripping blue.

: :

Painted shadows, blurry skies
with figures steeped in black.

Fuzzy lights that hypnotize..
an aphrodisiac.

: :

Couple meeting for a date,
Forty-eighth and Park.

Warm and wet, they conjugate
if hidden by the dark.

: :

Racing hearts in drizzled heat..
losing brolly, shoe.

Mirrors glaze a city street
as slicken voyeur's view.

Beasts

addition to the family

there's an egret in our field today

who shared with me his name
is Arthur..

follows our ponies, sifting
thru tracks for bugs
he might could

eat

::

his flock, I think, left
yesterday

his new best friend
Apache, seems

Arthur and Apache.. buds

egret and our
piebald

boy

as we, too

My landlord has a very happy and stubbornly old dachshund named Spikey.

He is smelly in his elder years, now relegated to a life outside their home. He in the doghouse, me in the nearby poolhouse. His eyes are milky and well impaired, ears mostly unhearing. Flea friendly and prone to itch, will scratch himself with vigor, encouraging you to do the same.

While landlord and family are sweet, it's clear they're waiting for Spikey's demise.. all ready for fresh and new and next. When father and kids comment on his rather notable longevity, it's never said with gratitude.

I see him in the morning from my bathroom window.. ambling about, bounding along on his short, little legs.. slanted in lean, prone to the left. Ever curious, facing the day like something he's never witnessed before.. boldly moving over here, bravely over there.. smelling this flower, sniffing that bug.

Sometimes I have to stop shaving and march right over, across the yard, past the pool, and hang with my bud. He slobbers on toes, I ask of his morn. Down on my knees and holding his face in my hands, I speak in the way flawed mortals do who love such beasts more than they should.

His big, cloudy eyes now beaming with pride.. my own, then, tending toward misty, too.

Keep on living and screw your folks..

　　　　and spend your time, what's left, with me.

believe he wanted berries..

July twenty-eighth

the Bear did appear..

> Was docile, would say,

> and still I knew fear.

He looked to my cows,

but not with a glare..

> Not hungry, I thought,

> as let go my scare.

Recalling the critters

I knew in my youth..

> All honey and bees,

> quite furry and cute.

I think he desired

to make a new bud..

Not tear me to shreds

nor lunch on my blood.

Much closer to Winnie,

the Pooh Bear of lore..

Just craving a friend,

and yet was unsure.

I passed him my sandwich

when felt for my knife..

Not *really* afraid

(as ran for my life).

http://www.youtube.com/watch?v=wQhCNOV5Gnk

Breakfast

(morning market)

Up on hind legs, proudly rose,
>   our yellow tabby's dance on toes.

En pointe as pointing ballet pose
>   for that fish there, not them nor those.

Paw to fin when nose to nose,
>   the ice is chilly, herrings froze.

Keeps them keen, won't decompose
>   as taste quite fresh, a pussy knows.

Reach and scoop 'til nigh enclose,
>   will glance around as breathing slows.

No one sees him, luck he owes
>   with meal in mouth.. away he goes.

Cauliflower Ear

Lost my Louie
  late last month,
not ready yet
   to mourn the boy.

Twenty-one years
  he warmed my head,
motorboat whirring
   as falling asleep.

Midnights are silent,
  drumless my dreams,
pillow beside me
   cold when I wake.

Timmy is gone
  as Louie now, too.
No butterscotch purrs,
   no love & be loved.

Someday, I vow,
  words I will write
and tell of his tale
   and tell of his tail.

Not now..

Lost my Louie
  late last month,
not ready yet
   to cry.

dream

sleepy cat on window sill
      both us yawning, morning still

me, afraid to start my day
      she, requests a rain delay

'stay in bed, I saw a cloud
      I will watch and purr quite loud..'

couldn't quarrel with her view
      slowing down and sleeping through

few more winks, her standing guard
      angel to her drowsy bard

'wake me at the crack of noon
      ere that hour, be too soon..'

Extra-Terrestrial

Alien with coldest nose,
    eyes as bugged as black abyss..

ears that dangled disappeared
    when catching frisbees, chasing bliss.

Whence he came I couldn't say
    as can't remember day or year.

But there he was like Christmastime
    and there he was when Beth appeared.

She and he, her own ET,
    the patient she would wrap and mend..

her teacup partner, dress-up puppy,
    favorite pillow, bestest friend.

Then boys arrived and shopping malls,
    all phones and proms and skinny jeans.

Less and less she needed him,
    his princess now a grown-up teen.

Yet when arriving home from college,
    holidays and summertime..

she'd ferry ET up the stairs,
    the ones he could no longer climb.

They'd carry on as if no time,
    she'd blabber campus gossip, stories.

Licked her face and half her toes,
    recounting golden frisbee glories.

Alien with bulging eyes
    grew slow and lean as time went by.

I don't remember when he left
    but do recall the way she cried.

importune

(in couplets)

as if were airbrushed, painted breeze
pied with colors, steeped in teas

whisks and whisps on fuzzy ear
eyes of doe, this tiny deer

pled with gaze for early nosh
bid her Dad, his chores awash

in penning, proofing, scribing prose
nuzzled prayer from tender nose

"Dearest Father, belly lacking
feed us with some gourmet snacking.."

yip and yelp to further ploy
sweetly sung to hedge annoy

"Child mine, too early lunch
perhaps a bite, a bit of brunch.."

two didst nibble sundry treats
lieu of meal, some orts and eats

followed by the smallest nap
folded Rosie in his lap

smile didst the writer beam
cradled baby, deep in dream

kitty meditations

(different days and times)

Trip to the kitchen, I pour a few more sips of joe in my cup.
Returning, I pass a ginger tom sitting in the cat tree.

His ears go back and flatten. Blinks his eyes as bows his head.

He suspects a drive-by kiss is in the offing..   and is not wrong.

My coffee tastes better.

::

I sit here writing. I should be asleep (graveyard shift tonight)
and not wondering why my butt hurts.

It occurs to me..

I've been perched for the last two hours on four inches of chair.

The rest occupied by a lion-sized, snoring brown tabby.

::

My roommate's white cat is very shy.. except with me.

Eating a rice cake the morning in question, I start typing (with
both hands), sticking the half-remaining biscuit in my mouth.

Angie wanders over and starts nibbling what's left dangling
over the keyboard.

The spacebar and several letters are sat upon, simultaneously.

My poem no longer rhymes.

Louie

(and chins)

A fine cat. CUT above. CUTE as heck.

With strawberry-blonde COAT
and
single-minded bearing...

had a broad face
and
ONE BLACK WHISKER

(every other one
white).

Stood OUT from the rest (even
UNDER your chair).

::

And absolutely NO ONE COULD
(nor ever should)

BUMP your chin
whilst walking nigh your KEYBOARD, strutting

with that same feline and feral
ferocity, fierceness
VELOCITY...

as he.

::

I dare say, before you finished that

PARTICULAR

paragraph, proofing...

he'd have left 6
TUFTS of orange FUR
there upon your mandible.

                              : :

Your profile NOW that of a man
with a GINGER tabby

VAN
DYKE.

Mojave Walk

(sunset)

AMBUSHED
on the rutted path,
circled by a
WAGON TRAIN.

4 WHITE WOLVES —
Mother, 3 grown Pups.

Licking, nipping, TASTING fingers.
PRAY that
I'm not PREY.

I'm not.

                    : :

MOM leads
scouting, reconnoiters.
2 PUPS follow,
me in tow —

as feel quite SAFE.

                    : :

THOMAS is
the only one who
leaves me know his NAME.
Brings up rear

and lets me pet him —

LEANING wolf against
my thigh

as STOP to watch the Sun go neath.

: :

He alone will WAIT —

me buying
GATORADE and maybe,
maybe

PUPPY BISCUITS improviso

at the only-one-for-miles
DESERT STORE / FILLING STATION.

: :

Walking home
all NIBBLES, SIPS —

both HOWLING up at Harvest Moon.

moth

not a fan of queuing up
        he held his ticket tight

looked aloft as sipped from cup
        whilst contemplating flight

knowing he was next in line
        mattered little, seems

his mettle set (as mulish mine)
        a tale of stubborn dreams

number called, no longer there
        no gripe nor formal plaint

pure as snow and canvas bare
        when leapt still lacking paint

for he and I had same intent
        airbrushed, neither nor

gathered colors where we went
        as flew through ever more

Night Anew

(forest eve)

A lowly one who knows his place,
          am happy living in my hole.

Permit me, please, to plead my case..
          a very ordinary mole.

After dark 'tis awfully rare,
          oh, less than 3 times 3, no doubt..

I've climbed a tree, presumed to stare,
          impatient 'til the stars will out.

But such a day and hour, this..
          when burning sol bedims, and then

the silhouetted pine abyss
          will welcome me and moon again.

random, years-apart L.B. musings

A tiny ladybug was wallowing upside down in a puddle on my balcony. I gently picked her up and carefully set her on a chair beneath the awning, protected from the morning rain. She is presently toweling off (having lent her the edge of a tissue).

I invited her to stay as long as she'd like, long as it's raining, long as she feels oozy.

::

And just like that, the left lens of my reading glasses skewed pink.

A ladybug had alit upon a corner, perfectly happy to assist me in writing this late afternoon.

::

There is a ladybug attending my yellow pad tonight. She seems too enamored of my desk lamp.

I worry for her future.

Smokey, Midnight, Annie

Foster Dad, the way I frame
        this never-meant-to-be
fatherless, and three could blame
        for fault doth lie with me

came to pass was given care
        of two who purred and drooled
third, a gift, a wolf so rare
        an angel, don't be fooled

::

tumult of the earthly kind
        warring factions fought
left with but a home to find
        penniless, was caught

loving was to lose my life
        leaving cutlass deep
pray to wrest this twisted knife
        a promise, could not keep

::

once again a Dickens' waif
        greyhound bus I board
Jesus, keep my babies safe
        I'll be fine, dear lord

cannot take what one can't tow
        when crippled is your cart
cannot feel what one can't know
        when broken is your heart

extempore am living now
                    lost and seldom found
left by those who disavow
                    to no one I am bound

please forgive a wounded soul
                    cloven, I am clad
love you three who made me whole
                    forever, Foster Dad

spun

'it's just a piece of yarn,' I said
and held it up to view

'maybe so, but tales I've read
claim magic in there, too..'

: :

and thus it settled, point resolved
we chanced upon a game

swish of thread, it didst evolve
to something far less tame

: :

the two of us, like Anime
cartoon cat and boy

flailing 'bout, a daft ballet
concerning yarn as toy

: :

wrote a score and sung it through
spirited, her part

little plot, but there in lieu
she stole my wool and heart

tender

dream of bunnies, *Lennie Small*
       and farm bucolic, pastoral

soften focus, phantoms purr
       when petting puppy's silken fur

pray I never harm with touch
       the every each I love too much

seeking words, I read again
       of Lennie's heart, *Of Mice and Men*

surplus vigor, brushing smooth
       as set on caring, solely soothe

please, Lord, let me curb my might
       to hug my babies, love just right

tiny rodents

(my inner bastard breathes)

make it so that I can read
   this simple-minded bloke

not a fancy, boring screed
    I fall asleep, awoke

give me meat or maybe pie
   to savor, sink my teeth

not scratch my head and wonder why
    there's too much crap beneath

plainer words and tighter text
   similes, a few

make me long to read what's next
    not wish I had a clue

so much stuff that's writ today
   is full of so much shit

no one reads it anyway
    before they can, they quit

I know, I do it all the time
   will read a verse or two

roll my eyes and comment I'm
    "so loving what you do"

people say the same of me
"dahhh-ling, oh your pen"

secretly and silently
they pray I'll not again

under those who write the worst
the comments stretch for days

and you can say you heard it first
right here.. I doubt their praise

lemmings follow lemmings who
when off the cliff they're flung

"god, you're good!" "I know, you too!"
as land in heaps of metered dung

winging

cold enough to worry for
the bunnies I can't
hug tonight

gather all beneath my fleece
to launch my cradle's
virgin flight

: :

in dreams we fly to Florida
by starlight ride my
trundle bed

have never flown a mattress bound
for warmer temps as
frost we fled

: :

quite worried that the pillow
won't be big enough
for every us

who'd like to rest our weary ears
whilst floating on this
futon bus

http://www.youtube.com/watch?v=goEDSnaDabg

wonderland, an epilogue

not the one you think it is
   our LEWIS CARROLL's.. loving his

     no, it's more a number two
       when magpie makes his BIG DEBUT

see, my mind is getting old
   as CAN'T REMEMBER things, I'm told

             : :

     birds that fly around our house
       all ravens, crows or OWLS, GROUSE..

BLACK and WHITE this other be
   the plot of tale escapeth me

     prequel, sequel "JABBERWOCKY"
       brillig, slithy toves too rocky

             : :

CLAUDE MONET, he painted snow
   his magpie on the fence, you know

     coalescing SETTING FOR..
       both Lewis, Claude's continued lore

Jabberwock and magpie beasts
   my SENSELESS WORDS for mimsy feasts

Colors

all day fun pass

(color me gay)

fair amount of time spent drinking
    maybe I'm insane
cerebellum small and shrinking
    Wonderland, my brain

Calliope's discordant sound
    shrill and out of tune
Ferris Wheel that lifts from ground
    when chasing after moon

horses on the Carousel
    alive and canter 'bout
Fortunetellers never tell
    prefer to twist and shout

cotton candy pink and blue
    Kewpie Doll, your prize
apples dipped in caramel glue
    mid swarm of hungry flies

clickety-clack of Coaster's wood
    no bar nor safety belt
Ice Cream cones that taste too good
    and mimic how I melt

ghostly Rides for holding hands
    mostly hold my own
Fun House mirrors, One-Man bands
    with me as all alone

Amusement Park in need of paint
    this Clown in need of nose
Carnie craving soul of saint
    lapel bereft of rose

float all day on feasting nights
    scarcely ever sleep
lost my mind in neon lights
    no lines, Admission cheap

anemic vs. wan

Republican as fiscal hawk
             BOTH sides mouth will gladly talk

if served their purpose, charmed their BASE
                    would sell their souls as saving face

: :

NO CORNER on the market, them
             Democrat, same stratagem

whichever side the other's on
                    will make a switch from PRO to CON

: :

CHOOSE a precept, dogma, creed
             not parlay votes for laud or greed

black is black and never white
                    flipping facts is NEVER RIGHT

Atlantis

(cyan shades)

Sky awash with seaweed sweet
if neath the ocean wave.

Swirls of beryl sweep the street
in sunken, turquoise grave.

Lost Marine of trident fame,
their God of naval gray.

Mythos spun with cobalt flame
as drowned by salty spray.

Mermen swim in lapis pools,
Aegean Sea below.

Singing Sirens, sapphire jewels
amidst the undertow.

Cerulean anemones,
azure-shaded hues.

Tiled relics, gold for free,
ruins wet with blue.

Catacombs of coral reef
for final resting place.

History of island, brief,
in watery embrace.

blending

sanguine blush of orchid mix
    in artery and vein

red and blue and florid wicks
    will burn the wax and wane

ebb and flow the clotted ooze
    as force the gobbets through

s_ck and f_ck the who you choose
    to bloody self be true

blue umbrella

she spied it by chance
  turned round in a glance

weather so fair
   when seeing it where

he noticed it too
  this perfectly new

umbrella in trash..
   was hers in a flash

   : :

she opened it plain
  invited the rain

impressionist town
   with wet coming down

strolling the street
  as ginger her feet

was wind in her hair
   now nearing him there

   : :

lacking an oar
  he tried to ignore

the squish in his shoes
   his rainy day blues

surprised from behind
'I pray you don't mind..'

some sharing begins
one brolly, two grins

: :

http://www.youtube.com/watch?v=RncvCSS1lL4

DRIPS

Was trying to remember
when I first determined BLUE and GREEN
were my favorite
colors.

I may have been 8.

GREEN striped BELL BOTTOMS
pulled up Steve Urkel high...
BLUE hand-me-down corduroy shirt
with sleeves too short.

I wavered somewhere between
The PARTRIDGE FAMILY
and Don Knotts.

::

But what does this have to do with the
title of the Poem.. 'DRIPS'?

I'm not sure.. but maybe they remind me of certain
of-a-color reflections...

WATER DROPS
by a lake I once swam in..
coming off Linda's GREEN BIKINI,
beneath the BLUE SKY
of a 14-year-old's
first date.

Lucky drips.

Gilded

(lacking)

Halcyon of FEATHERED FLAKE,
this picture frame like frosted cake.

GOLDEN SLUMBERS, plated scroll
of metal flourish, inlaid knoll.

: :

Splendid yellow, TAWNY GLAZE,
its tinsel trimming set ablaze

BY FILIGREE of ribboned plaque,
appliqué with braided back.

: :

Set in kiln as TRINKET TOOLED
mid arabesques and flounces pooled.

WHAT, PRAY TELL, to place within
my empty mount of fancy skin..

GREEN APPLE

(René Magritte)

THUSLY TRUE, the fruit appeared..
needed then, in fact, be steered

    for compromised, forever was
    my seeing... WHAT AN APPLE DOES

        : :

in front of face, still hovering..
my MOUTH and NOSE, still covering

    is ever-tricky EATING PIE
    with less assistance, aid from eye

        : :

knotty too, ESPECIALLY..
when snogging someone flesh-ily

    as LICKING LOBES will never rate
    the joy it used to stimulate

        : :

now, whenever MAKING LOVE...
kissing things below, above

    I find my tongue of little use
    for OUT MY LIPS comes apple juice

http://www.renemagritte.org/the-son-of-man.jsp

IN CONCERT

(mulatto)

Twixt the flats and sharps there lay
     the purest notes a hand could play.

     With keys bereft of blush or stain,
          are clean of timbre, tint.. remain.

Ebony seems add the flash
     as set above a pearly cache.

     Black & White are eighty-eight
          in harmonies we orchestrate.

MIMIC VIEW

       seldom is there
SYMMETRY
       left to right or
UP & DOWN

       dusty luster
SILVER SHADES
       fly and dive me
MIRROR SIDE

       swimming under
MINUS BREATH
       strangely still alive
CAN SEE

       six feet under
ECHOES BACK
       silver too
ASLEEP

       what above is
SAME BELOW
       minus rhyme as
PATTER SHINES

neutral

what if ALL is this and that
      half I drooled and some I spat

split between the sea and sky
      nothing far and little nigh

life detached and nonchalant
      not well fed but not quite gaunt

middle riding center line
      kinda lousy, sorta fine

: :

what if GOD is somewhat good
      something less than understood

disengaged from Babylon
      views his children with a yawn

all the noble mixed with bad
      cancels out, a greyish plaid

fair and measured, mostly tame
      beauty, crudeness all the same

: :

what if SUN is only warm
      tepid rays and cool the norm

nothing like the blaze that bakes
      often taking coffee breaks

end of day and end of light
     same as every other night

half and half and maybe less
     apathy we acquiesce

overlay in glaze

gauzy folds of hazy hues
       ombre shades that blend and fuse

lazy brush would rather snooze
       wavy lines that almost ooze

of the colors, which to choose
       love this range of rainbow views

jot of jazz as lumens muse
       ink in quill is black with blues

pink

funny split I like to eat
  to savor, tangy, bittersweet

aftertaste on tongue and tip
  of yes indeed, that thing I slip

                    : :

inside with all that warm and tight
  is adding to her wet tonight

sipping neath and round the folds
  lapping liquids, all she holds

                    : :

dripping drops amidst, among
  her hardened nib to match my hung

deep within I leave my own
  when pink now creamy.. seed I've sown

pride in color

Can you let me be the me I think I am?

I will never hurt you with my pronouns.
I will never harm you with my melanin.

I will never hack you with

my dress, my drink,
my womb, my wish

to live my life as I see fit..

as I wish same for you.

Random Forest

(haiku pine)

Bound in moss and bark,

    fir trees rising stoic, stark.

    Fast approaching dark.

Almost out of sight,

    velvet rabbit, dying light.

    Snaking branches fight.

Summer solstice gleans,

    drenched in twilight's in-between.

    Night of evergreen.

sniffle

the renegade of rainbow hues
oddest cast of green
    took a stand in platform shoes
arrived by limousine

'autographs, I've not a lot
apologies, I've none
    and if I look akin to snot
I've only just begun'

: :

a fugitive from malachite
beryl, olive, moss
    spinach he would gladly fight
hated pesto sauce

for in his life, a verdant sea
full of tone and tint
    rejected leaf and lime and pea
and every shade of mint

: :

forest, teal and willow bice
apple, sage and jade
    eschewed them all as not too nice
ugly each, their shade

excepted phlegm, his color class
please remember this
    brown he ain't from no one's ass
nor lemon yellow piss

               : :

but sneeze that spits from loaded nose
the spatter that we spew
    hock a loogie, could suppose
all lovely tasting goo

Kardashian of human juice
celebrity of ooze
    same the flavor, me or moose
'tis mucus mine I choose'

Spring

LIME and Moss from GOLDEN Fleece,
        TANGERINE to Rose Cerise..

Apple Red for BLUSHING Pink,
        FUCHSIA flush with ORCHID's ink.

OMBRE streaks on taffy SWEET,
        Cotton Candy FUZZY, eat..

Brightest tints in AFTERGLOW,
        SUNSET Beaches, Mexico.

Awnings STRIPED throwing SHADE,
        Picnic Blankets, PLAID on glade..

SHERBET dripping, sticky fingers,
        MAY in bloom as TIE-DYE lingers.

tiny gamut

spare me but a little grace
permitting if I err

    tween us is but breathing space
    as you and I compare

shades of colors as I grew
blended more to gray

    black and white no longer new
    with rigid giving way

: :

nuanced musings fill my soul
pearl to charcoal tints

    folded in a sausage roll
    all whispered thoughts and hints

extremities of yay or nay
simple answers sate

    too, too often what they say
    perceived as love or hate

: :

noooooo, 'tis but a notion dense
if see the other side

    as enemy to making sense
    is compromise denied

simple case of how we view
complexities in life

    when clashing casts of me and you
    mix well with palette knife

Vincent

Sophomore class,
    Power Memorial Academy
        Catholic High School for Boys.

           Handsome face scarred by acne,
        not much older than us,
        Mr. Franzetti

tried to impart
    a love for words
        on diffident ears.

           Unremarkable day,
        third week in May,
        walked into class

not with his
    normal texts and books
        and rumpled papers splayed,

           but carried a child's hi-fi player
        (was red, I recall) and a
        small vinyl disc.

Silently,
    he set it all down,
        outlet was found, needle placed

on spinning black plastic.
Don McLean's
VINCENT

as static spit first
then waves of a verse.
Teacher on podium leaned into class,

searching our faces for
glimmers of grasping.
His eyes welling up,

brow now dappled
with fever dream beads
all hoping the paint and poetry sung,

lyrics of hope and despair,
would touch us inside
same it did him.

And he, for that time,
was Vincent, too.. cautioning
those who carried the gene that tempts

to set one's skies ablaze
with thick violet haze
and not simply blue..

there was someone
like you who knew how it felt,

daubing in shades of shadowy hues.

Omens not stone. No standing alone.
Gray palette clouds, no tragic
demise need thusly arise.

Now I think
I know what you
tried to say to me...

One of your boys replays that day
when starry, starry nights
allow for no sleep.

http://www.youtube.com/watch?v=dipFMJckZOM

whitish

cold is first that comes to mind
a sylvan field in snow

firn and ice as intertwined
or close-up glacier floe

: :

gauzy silk for sheerest blouse
my love exposed beneath

I'd nary let her leave the house
more gossamer than sheath

: :

pixel from a random star
one of trillions spied

luminous in flux afar
alit and magnified

: :

glare that glows from modern lamp
squarely cubed its base

fulgent watts of light and amp
through ashen shade of lace

: :

or maybe just a window pane
one frosty early morn

soon be clear with April's rain
when vernal bis is born

: :

hard to know the image true
this piece of tone on tone

canvas craving green and blue
or veins in marbled stone

Ego

ANGRY

I hate THAT and can't stand THIS
      as full of rage and bursting piss.

All those there, they all suck..
      everyone's a STUPID FUCK.

Even YOU'RE a piece of shit..
      asshole, douche bag, hypocrite.

Rancid verse and words that smell
      when poets tell us.. GO TO HELL.

I'LL ALLOW each bard to write
      one such poem spewing spite.

More than that, I must confess..
      you sound the FOOL, do not impress.

If you'd like to FIX what's broke..
      kill with clever, don't provoke.

Inspire me with words of change,
      BEND my thinking.. rearrange.

because I care

snivel not
without a fight

to lift your lot in life

woe is me
is fucking old

go grab an eager knife

cut the crap
carve and cleave

the rot that leads to reek

shut your hole
as fix what's broke

to be the keen you seek

Bidding

BRILLIANT is the way I think
                    yes, it's true, my shit don't stink

my poems GRAND.. call it swagger
                    call me what I am... a braggart

every thought so WELL-EXPRESSED
                    clearly, I've been sonnet blessed

hubris is my middle name
                    if Karma bites, I'll take the BLAME

BUT WHEN it comes to thoughts *you* pose
                    opining verse and gifting prose

it seems you're LACKING paper, quill
                    no goals you share nor dreams you spill

are witless memes the WHOLE you've got..?
                    asks modest me, so shrinking, not

how about a word or two
                    on how *you* feel.. not others... *YOU*

BLINDS

(film noir)

I feel more at EASE,
　　　　the ladies I please,

INTREPID in tux,
　　　　though nothing deluxe

nor ever too tight
　　　　(is LOOSE for a fight)..

worn with a VEST
　　　　protecting my best,

stopping the lead
　　　　when keeping the RED

flowing WITHIN
　　　　and under my skin.

　　　　　　: :

Of course, there's a GUN,
　　　　this favorite son

can SHOOT off a flake
　　　　(the care that I take),

the dandruff that falls
　　　　and lands on the BALLS

of perps who will lie..
　　　　in JAIL they'll deny

if ever confronted
      on why they look STUNTED..

will feel like a dope
      when DROPPING the soap.

         : :

And then there's my BOAST,
      more James Bond than most,

who thinks he INVENTED
      (in fact he just rented)

my STYLE and grace
      but never my face,

for surely that's mine..
      OH YES, he's done fine,

but I've got the height,
      look better at NIGHT,

too handsome for hats
      when PEEKING out slats.

de novo

(thinning liquids)

Not felt this way for many years.. reawakened dormant fears, enabled hate to sluice through veins.. syrup-seeping pores unplugged, treacle with ink.

With pen I think.

::

Before unclabbered system cloyed.. undestroyed, could not conceive of even just.. the thought that this was clearly what I loathed.

I am unclothed.

::

I rouse the sallowed, heretofore, unhallowed knave.. as coma swathed a strangled soul.. anewly wakened, spit replacing thickened blood and tears with piss.

Heart above abyss.

::

Stirred to sweat tween acid raindrops, dripping burnt and learnt I plot.. scorn the ones who even air as simple thing as whispered doubt.. this is what I'll do.

They're through.

DIVIDE

(morning subway, no one sees)

Paper covers, scissor cuts,
  rock breaks shears as reason shuts.

Bury heads behind a guise
  as fixate focus, downcast eyes.

Boomers blame Millennials
  when young'uns and Centennials

get their news in different ways.
  All pupils blurring. Bleary gaze.

Fingers licked and pages turned
  or content scanned and circuits burned..

Both result in severed bonds.
  Smartphone, paper... look beyond.

Familiar

(2024)

SIMILE, it could be said,
Russian hookers, PISS-SOAKED BED.

      Golden Showers, ORANGE SKIN,
      FOX AND FRIENDS and full of spin.

Scrub the mattress, spray FEBREZE,
kill the STENCH, will make you sneeze.

      ALL OF THIS and still I think
      where'er he lays is BOUND TO STINK.

heretic

(my friend enjoins)

Who is this God so insecure, *so hungry for prayers*

(too innocent and elegant, in eloquence he
queried, English as a second
language),

that He makes us jump thru hoops
and clamber peaks to
please Him?

I DO not ask such things
of friends

nor beasts and plants beneath my care...

to only be exactly who they
(at that moment)

are.

: :

For that (alone) I love them.

huckster

pretend you're not too fabulous
act as if you're shy

humble, simple, sweetly thus
a quiet kind of guy

: :

never will they call on you
to lead them into fight

stay thee safe in endless queue
with ego small and slight

: :

secure you will forever be
if nary ask for much

'please, don't look too close at me'
recoil from their touch

: :

hasn't worked as yet, my ploy
now I choose to yell

pay attention to this boy
is loud.. *the soul I sell*

is you

stay the one who does you harm
but what if HE grabs same
YOUR arm..

who will hold the other's fist
and who betray with
Judas' kiss?

::

catch a thief who steals as ghost
but what if SHE is same
YOUR host..

who will serve their time in jail
and who collect our
felon's bail?

::

stake the heart of soul possessed
but what if BLOOD is from
YOUR breast..

who will close the open wound
and who will live in hell
marooned?

::

burn the eyes that leer with sin
but what if THEY look
deep WITHIN..

who will see what others see
when scalded orbs look
back at thee?

: :

murder he that murders who
but what if THEY are
merely YOU..

who will fill the flowered grave
and who will weep for
no one saved?

needed

there but for the rotten stuff
and chafe in every day

      where but for the failures rough
      that vex along the way

self would never be so tough
to temper feet of clay

      soul would never see enough
      perceive the white in gray

Nom de Plume

Secrets simmer 'neath the skin,
       bubble up from DEEP WITHIN.

Wonder whether call it sin,
       NEVER LYING — only spin.

Yet with sneaky, STEALTHY STRIDE,
       footsteps furtive, words belied.

PRIVATE PEN and mannered pride
       — poems cloaked and classified.

Avatar might make you think,
       clever chap with HIDDEN INK.

Well I know as had my drink —
       TASTY VERSE with trace of stink.

one beach

(first time model)

perfect hour, perfect light
'til early twilight, nigh the night

    sand was wet but warm enough
    water frothy, not too rough

as laid before the churning sea
tried my best to not be me

       : :

    not be boy with frightened stare
    not be kid with skin too fair

not be runt with scrawny arms
not be boor bereft of charms

    not be fag with hair too long
    not be loser ever wrong

       : :

not be punk with pouty lips
not be twink with skinny hips

    not be scared of things I feared
    not be geek with thoughts too weird

not be freak who cried too much
not be misfit begging touch

       : :

for one brief moment, fate did smile
along one beach, one ocean mile

golden lad who not yet man
now lying down, afraid to stand

pretty face if not too smart
was posing with a lonely heart

http://www.facebook.com/photo?fbid=10150091349604763

PERFECT

thereupon, I sussed it out
when started making sense..
   whispered mumble led to shout
and lightened what was dense

flawless is a liquid thing
as Bible tells us so
   Sea of Red didst part and bring
the Jews along in tow

from the Old and through the New
their God was absolute
   perfect, purely peerless, true
infallibly astute

: :

and yet, He changed from smite to kiss
Leviticus to John
   letting go of wrath and piss
His Son did focus on..

something new, was perfect, still
a Testament of Love
   faultless now defined at will
Death replaced by Dove

surely, this is proof enough
that paradigms can shift
   what was full of huff and puff
can morph and change to drift

: :

often I will pray to Him
(sometimes I will yell)
        tell Him things are trending grim
this life that tends toward hell

    will homilize my humble views
trying not to snap
        'MAY I TELL YOU, RIGHTEOUS MUSE
PERFECT? *FULL OF CRAP!'*

    out the mouth of babes, the phrase
is how I hope I'm heard
        'Dude, you need to change your ways
or redefine that word..'

salesman

unashamed and unrepentant, simply
didn't care... those who thought me
ill-equipped caught wholly unaware

    answer wasn't black or white, rather
    pointless gray...   kind of tweed with
    weft and weave, a sort of shadow play

        juxtaposed against it all, a stubborn
        Taurus streak...   bulls are not a timid
        beast as rarely leaning meek

through the room I cut a path yelling
out my name...   priming folks be well-
advised of soon my coming fame

    offered each my pearly whites, a selfie
    rife with me...   tell your kids how proud
    you were, a fanboy devotee

        rapt in your adoring eyes, I understand
        them well...   after all, is me you fancy

...least the one I sell

shoe

I no longer have a grasp on reality
moving through Life as

I do..

    is all but proof I'm daft.

      : :

I read your words and think,
'I can write better.'

And maybe I can..

    but what does it matter if I can't feed myself?

      : :

How ironic, you with a home and me not..

all the while thinking
I'm so

    talented.

      : :

Yet..

how does being humble, noble
and precious

    sell my words?

SUPERMAN BEANIE

I'll never try, pretend to be,
    a SUPERHERO type... not me.

Never fly with BILLOWED CAPE
    nor hope to be in better shape.

I LIKE pajamas, mostly plaid,
    in TIGHTS I look distinctly bad.

Especially if RED and BLUE,
    the ones he wore, the times he flew.

Superman had MUSCLED PECS,
    people ask me not to flex.

FASTER than a bullet fired,
    me... I'm feeling old and tired.

Locomotive, STRONGER, SPEEDING,
    think I'm only tough when reading.

Save the day with X-Ray Sight,
    DOUBTFUL I would last the night.

Yet, I have a KNITTED CAP
    and like to wear it when I nap.

I DREAM I rescue Lois Lane,
    am swifter than a zooming plane.

Kryptonite might do me in,
  still the BAD GUYS never win.

In my beanie, Man of Steel,
    SAVING WORLD has great appeal...

Then & Present

(archeological dig)

Three of us upon on a rock,

    reliving *now* as ancient past.

Never thought that day would end

    as never dreamed their love would last.

College flings and studied things,

    forgot the *history* yet amassed.

Two were paired with me alone,

    regret the answers never asked.

triple threat

I define myself, most often, as an ARTIST. It's what I do in my day-job as textile designer. It's what I did as a kid with construction paper and magic markers.

While I never was a gifted illustrator, never one to draw that well, I always had a good sense of graphics, color, content.

Can work with shadows, shapes and shades.. and layer them cleverly in Photoshop.

::

Similarly, I'm an ACTOR. Instead of wielding paint and brush, software programs, Epson ink..

I use myself, my soul, my face as canvas, crayon, catalyst.

Become a palette.. maybe leaning gray.

::

Then I started writing. AUTHOR wanting more.

Now I pen the scenes and script, film the action, twist the plot, paint the backdrops, act all roles.. and walk the carpet red.

Plying only black and white.

::

ARTIST, ACTOR, AUTHOR.. easels. Only colors change.

http://www.youtube.com/watch?v=I52eefwAKDE

weigh

breath between the sane, insane
  but tiny gust of wind

as I age, the poise I feign
  is stripped of wit and skinned

query this unwieldy sort
  if whether sound of mind

lucid thoughts with clear comport
  or brain now misaligned

fact is, likely, both are true
  our wisdom comes with cuts

slash and spread and slice right through
  for all of us are nuts

Family

2 Sons, 2 Dads

fitful breeze of wheeze and sputter
Father kneels before
a grave

years of smoking LUCKY STRIKES
gravel-throated rosary as

sonnet for his Son

: :

pieces of this boy, fragments
bones now buried
plot beneath

felled as well by LUCKY STRIKE

different kind, no cigarette, an IED
crammed with shards
placed by Son

another
Son

who loved his Dad the same as first

afterword

Puff the legend epilogue
      Jackie Papers' final blog —

anon, I came to see the light
      how dragon needs a boy for flight

returned to then and there, beheld
      a frightened reptile sorrow felled

eyes grew wet when meeting mine
      as tail swung round me serpentine

              : :

by my side, my son stood still
      beast and boy both mute until..

something new and something old
      recalling fancy stories told

autumn mist and dragon's lair
      now coming home with fabled heir

I searched his den for boat and sail
      espied the scars on scales and tail

              : :

the painted wings and giants' rings
        with ceiling wax and magic strings

were missing from his humble cave
                though knew his heart and soul yet brave

my son looked up with nearly grin
            as roar of three didst nigh begin —

fire breathing, Puff did plea
                and all flew off to Honahlee

: :

http://www.youtube.com/watch?v=z15pxWUXvLY

BAKING

I think back
   REMEMBER —

MOM never
   smiled without
chocolate icing
   smeared on her teeth

licking ten fingers —

the end of making
   a CHOCOLATE CAKE

never had less
   than a fistful of flour
stuck to the sweat
   of her brow —

after such
   an endless ENDEAVOR

with mixer
   never so BROWN

           : :

my Mom was real —

a Donna Reed dud
   when following RULES —

batter and icing
   always well-sampled

off spatula, spoon

her drooling boys
   watching AGHAST —

eternally waiting
   in pain and impatient 'til
finally —
   FINALLY —

bowls went to us

Booth

War was over, fears allayed,
her soldier due by noon..

    Three whole years, a world away,
    at last their honeymoon.

: :

Meet and eat and toast their life
with railway diner fare..

    Celebrating husband, wife,
    a cuppa joe, a prayer.

: :

Not at home, she missed the call,
out shopping for a hat..

    Bought a purse with shoes and shawl,
    a vision where she sat.

: :

Came his train as came the next,
one never-ending line..

    Stayed her grin, her smile flexed
    as never asked the time.

: :

Ordered lunch, enough for two,
when barely took a bite..

    Stared at dinner, whistle blew
    and shook a silent night.

chrysalis

not to be pressed 'tween pages of book
    nor to be hung from branches or hook

fallen and captured, raptured on high
    unraveling ripe, not ready to fly

wings in a furl, pupa concealed
    hidden behind a window, revealed

born to be good, kept as a child
    craving the life her parents thought wild

loving a man who pounded her shell
    breathless and moaning, a passage to hell

fire did singe the tips of her wings
    living the flame, the sizzle it sings

fragile no more, a beast from within
    his quivering heart now piercing her skin

never looked back as never entombed
    crystal was shattered, antennae ungroomed

lovely she floats on a butterfly's kiss
    cursed by the Church and living in bliss

daisy chain

Mason jars whose early life
     held jelly canned by farmer's wife.

Sold at market, berry filled,
     pectin scooped and spread and spilled.

Empty glasses clean and clear
     enlisted next for serving beer.

From steins of ale to lading paint
     for brushing stencils, colors quaint.

To heirloom vases sold at store,
     our farmer's wife, she bought all four.

They traveled far as rambled, roamed,
     now holding flowers..   back at home.

FORWARD

(line of ape to man)

not a race we ever win

in Evolution's discipline

Eden's garden, naked skin

God doth punish early sin

changeling view from pelvic fin

swim and crawl to walking kin

inventor fire, wheels that spin

science, tech.. let chase begin

ever faster, spread too thin

fate has ways of cutting in

to slow the relay, stop the din

look behind... another twin

Friday Morning

13 hours, 3 minutes

on Amtrak's SOUTHWEST CHIEF..

with me crossing from Albuquerque, NM
to Victorville, CA.. the train
continuing
onto Los Angeles.

Was like the PBS Specials
I watched, stoned, 25 years ago...
programs on GREAT TRAINS that used to

traverse America.

Passenger Cars with windows
above and all around.. LIGHT pouring in.

Dads in ties and Moms in circle skirts...

LEAVE IT TO BEAVER noses glued to WINDOWS.

::

Clearly, I was on a Ghost Train.

What I BEHELD that Thursday looked the same

as the rarefied snippets of News Reel footage strewn together
by Public TV..

when found me, 25 years earlier, open-mouthed and
DROOLING on my bed...

reveling in those (thankfully) short-lived, "my God
everything is sooo interesting",

oxycodone days.

: :

These were Membership Drive broadcasts I then
purchased for my Dad...

hoping he'd find them as THRILLING as his
doped-up offspring.

He did.

: :

Son, no longer subject to the WHIMS
of chemical alterings,

is STILL so very powerless against
the remarkable frailty
of SPLENDOR..

when time and space and speeding locomotive BESTOW
then RESCIND, over and over,

their Gifts.

I am again slack-jawed and slavering.

: :

Boarded with
4 and 1/2 hours of DAYLIGHT left.

There were VISTAS, that remaining afternoon, I was not
prepared for nor dreamed could ever be like....

as NO ONE expects the WHAT they expect
to actually, actually be.

But there they were too endlessly..
even better, oh my Lord,
more BEAUTIFUL than THAT
I saw on PBS TV.

: :

Trust me, Trump,

America is.. and always was...
GREAT.

: :

It was the longest SUNSET EVER
witnessed (with train and sun both moving west).
I was sitting in the
Observation Car with

the youngest Old Lady I ever had the pleasure...

still a traveling Rock Band Groupie
and all-around GORGEOUS
Spiritual Whore..

with whom I made some small (HUGE) talk of
cotton candy, photographs and
pleasant folks who morph
to monsters

given too much wine.
As loved her for that hour sipping,

maybe now a little, too.

(LOVE THEM ALL, but seems
too short to love
them as I do..   but do.)

: :

Couldn't sleep..

Envied the rich Dining Car folk and
Sleeping Car patrons,

and children who paraded noisily
between the two...

: :

Think I've written ENOUGH.

The clickity-clack bespoke of Dad. We hugged.
He forgave..

I'm not sure for what.

I flew for a minute with JESUS, I slept for seconds/years,
landing there in VICTORVILLE.

: :

Another spirit, maybe an Angel,
one in tiny denim shorts..
snuggest tank top

made me Breakfast.

(Why are
Angels

so lovely?)

Speaking of Jesus
(and what He would do)...

the SAME with her
as me,

I'm
  sure..

Hijab

Taahirah never dreamed therapy could effect such relief. Dr. Kyrie's mantra did miracles to quell her panic attacks.

She'd close her eyes and imagine a crossbow pulled taut, ready to release its feathered shaft. The target always changed. The fervor of her defense did not.

9 words.

"I am not a woman. I am a warrior."

: :

Readied, aimed and fired... the flint-tipped, quilled and quivering missiles never missed their allegoric mark. Behind the armor of a wrapped veil, she was anonymous. Her symbolic enemies slain by an unseen, merciless foe.

How does he?

Far beyond the walls of her psychiatrist's office, no longer cocooned by his comfortable couch, she still found strength in those 12 English syllables. 23 Western letters.

Allahu Akbar! He wasn't even a Muslim! A secular shrink, who married a Jew, who celebrates Christmas.

She was raised to believe in many things. A woman's strength was not one of them. Even the lore of Nusaybah bint Ka'ab, companion and shield of Prophet Muhammad, was a mythos she could not relate.

Her new country felt strange and sinister. Their music.. obscene. Freedoms.. repugnant. Worship of women.. profane. And humor.. blasphemous. They were infidels cursed and deserving of death.

And yet...

Here is this Doctor so antithetical to Sharia dogma, counter to the precepts put forth by her Imam, ignorant of the Qur'an, incompatible with her beliefs in sacred Islam.

How does he?

To wit.. equip her so handily, armed with the munitions of a simple, empowering phrase... weaponry to master her trembling. Her phobia of flying, defeated.

At last, able to return her Father's body to the place of his birth.

: :

But what daughter, what Jinn from Jahannam, would question Muhammad's decrees?

Women are but half of men's worth, fields to be plowed, struck when defiant, the bulk of the dwellers in Hell.

And what wicked dybbuk could deliver such blows to the fears that kept her submissive.. recumbent before the hand of a Father, locked within a linen shroud? Protected/imprisoned by both.

How does he?

But without Dr. Kyrie's 9 words, she could never lay her Father to rest.

Dishonor him to honor him.

:	:

Unflinching, Taahirah boarded the plane, her Father's bathed and wrapped remains lading below. She whispered his Janazah prayer, praying for forgiveness.

Smiled, remembering her therapist's eyes. Smiled again at the thought of meeting her cousins waiting for her at the Cairo airport. Feeling blessed by Allah.

Unsure if she was worthy... now tainted by Western ideals.

:	:

She pondered these things willingly, conflicted yet happy with the progress she had made pinning her sincerely held beliefs to a future that promised even more, if contrite, enlightenment.

All this splendid Aufklärung as the plane silently, stealthily descended into the side of a mountain. Was brought to a fiery end by a stranger on board.. his unsheathed and secreted jambiya at the pilot's throat.

The passenger, another devout Muslim, wrestling with his own spiritual riddles.

:	:

http://www.youtube.com/watch?v=tLzBENQ3Ii8

LIFT

(a Mom's past)

Happy she had straightened her seams that morning. Happy to have stockings at all. The War was particularly hard on a girl with legs that stretched out long as Margaret's.

And with skirts now shorter, skimming the knee (more collateral damage from the BLITZKRIEG and its ensuant fabric rationing), was a lot more real estate to swathe in nylon, a lot more backyard runway to keep lined and lit.. a lot more naked to feel when one had to go without.

GAMS..

The Holy Grail of Betty Grable. And though our gal would never be similarly emblazoned the side of a B-17, she felt a kinship with Betty's rump, fondness for Hollywood in general, the boys overseas, a newly promoted Jimmy Stewart. And the thought of being his real-life Donna Reed, starring in their own of-course-it-could-happen variant of IT'S A WONDERFUL LIFE, looped round and round her inner Newsreel *despite* the film having yet been made.

: :

She had ever-endeavored to keep the back of her legs seamed, the landing strip striped and visible. I mean, it was a well-known fact Bob and Bing liked their girls in TIGHT SWEATERS and UNTWISTED HOSE. Just ask Miss Lamour and her deftly applied lipstick.

For Margaret, with her moxie for keeping such lists..
was check, check (and check).

And subbing mascara for a nylon-tucked seam? Couldn't draw

a straight line even with the Führer's Luger held tight to her temple. Her calf would end up looking like the coastline of Normandy *after* the Invasion.

Was a dame's duty to stay fit for battle, ship-shape, keep 'em flying high (where the tight sweaters came in handy), GIVE 'EM SOMETHING TO FIGHT FOR, something to come home to..

: :

By the 34th floor, the lift had been whittled down to a scant three. The ancient mariner in glasses and snood sailed out onto the building's secretarial pool floor, leaving just two. Doors closed on the tapping, typing din.

Ding of the elevator promised silence.

She'd seen him before, John Powers, purportedly famous model agent, probably huckster. Anyone involved with luring young career gals into the lascivious life of a STARLET MODEL CELEB must have ulterior motives. Still, glad she took the extra time to neaten her seams that AM.

Turning toward the wall of the wobbly Otis elevator, knew she had but twelve more floors to feign picking at the fake wood laminate, brandish her calves, carefully swaying her back that smidge more than usual, lifting a caboose ever-so-slightly. With A-line skirt stretched taut over hips, her left heel seemed swept up as it rose with bent knee, like Ginger Rogers mid spin.

: :

"HAVE YOU EVER MODELED?"

Having already thought long and hard about even the *notion* of such a question, she pursed her dewy lips, continuing her sham examination of the paneling, still all wrapped up in her Betty Grable posturing.

Two floors later, hands on hips, peering over a shoulder pad, she replied as if *just now* catching his query.

"WHY NO.. I'VE NOT."

Lying wasn't easy for a good, Irish Catholic girl, adding this fib to the list she'd prattle off to Father O'Connor come Saturday.

"ARE MY SEAMS STRAIGHT?" she deigned to inquire.

And with her own question still pendulous, she exited the lift. Amid a well-executed toss of her tresses, stopped but a foot and a half in front of the soon-to-be closing doors, shimmied and fussed with her garter belt right through her skirt (with no such adjustment seemingly needed).

Sensing an audience, her head turned profile.

"HOW VERY DARE YOU.." managing a wink and withering smile as the doors clipped shut.

: :

Checking her watch, swore to herself she'd be on that same elevator tomorrow, doubtless at that same time, and likely every day thereafter.

Lunch hours would find her firmly fixated, fiendishly focused, fishing in Wanamaker's hosiery department.

: :

http://www.youtube.com/watch?v=vQGt4XwwFsc

mailbox midst the pines

(bird has found a roof)

cathedral-vaulted dome

    hallowed home, needle nesting

havened from the rain

missing flap and flag

    archway open, flutter of

mama bearing food

babies lieu of mail

    numbers now unreadable

house upon a post

New Friend

(Godfrey H.)

Zeitgeist shared with billow, swoon,
      your leafy shade allowing moon.

Some might say a twin-speak thing,
      our budding bromance, blaming Spring?

Great minds think (and drink) alike,
      while mine seems on a long-ass hike.

Maybe yours makes up for me
      when side by side.. I like your tree.

not the same

   reminds me of another tree
another verse I penned
   but not alike, I swear to thee
on this I'll never bend

   every branch, I'm crystal clear
with timber nary same
   every twig and leaf is dear
a metaphor, I claim

   though similar in many ways
you and I... 'tis true
   I'm sure I sense a deeper craze
when looking back at you

   maybe not too sane myself
abed, I need to rest
   but there above, upon the shelf
my anger, unexpressed

   fear me not and laugh it off
perhaps I've had a drink
   not too close, I nurse a cough
nigh, I'm on the brink

   of telling you the truth, I hold
the end is likely near
   yesterday my soul I sold
so sit beside me ...here

NUMERICAL

It fell upon a SATURDAY,
I found the key to breath.

Simple figures, easy way,
a TRIUMPH over death.

: :

All I did was flip the fraction,
LIFE and LOVE reversed.

Divide the two by this reaction..
LOVE is always first.

: :

Many years I worked the NUMBERS,
stumped by all the fuss.

All the MATH we use encumbers,
separating us..

: :

Friday night, the EVE BEFORE,
laying down, I slept.

Woke by BROTHER banging door,
when on my shoulder wept.

: :

Father passed that early morn,
I NEVER said goodbye..

adding up a SOUL REBORN,
subtracting when we die.

: :

ALGEBRAIC quotient clever,
calculations done.

Dad and I would stay FOREVER..
2 in heart, as 1.

one side – other

Support for DACA, we have room.
> *But what of DREAMERS ripped from womb?*

Saving CHILDREN here since birth.
> *But killing FETUS deemed no worth.*

Funding HEALTH CARE, not your fight.
> *But what of NEWBORN's wellness plight?*

Less ABORTION, I'm with you.
> *But help for MOTHER not your view.*

No more laws to govern GUNS.
> *But what of shooting DAUGHTERS, SONS?*

Schools and KIDS, we need protect.
> *But NRA wants rules unchecked.*

SAME

Now she's headed TOWARD the sound,
     this time louder, shook the ground.

Rumbled deeper, distant knell.
     Running faster, RACING, fell —

Not afraid of what AWAITS,
     gasping, grasping, tempting fates.

Death or worse could be denied
     if fighting, FUCK 'EM — fortified.

: :

Gathered WEAPONS as she flew,
     sticks and stones, her fingers knew.

Chances slender stirred her pique.
     Flying BLINDLY promised bleak —

NO surrender, not a night
     for ceding, folding, NEVER flight.

Fight a FOE, no more she'd flee
     from fire-breathing — be set free.

: :

There, beyond the burning brush,
     softer bellows, SWEETER hush.

Baby SWADDLED nary burned.
     Dragon leaving once more turned —

Eyes of two now closely twinned
       as tears of both are BLAMED on wind.

Serpent stumbles — cradles own.
       MOTHERS' TRUCE as grace is sown.

SPAN

From here
to there is so much
lake,
no bridge above the piss..

The sun
behind a sallow
wake,
of old I reminisce.

::

Once
upon a time that
ends
with money in my hand..

Slipped
thru fingers serving
friends
like sifting, shifting sand.

::

I pray
for but a tiny
loan,
no way across I see..

Modest
boat to bring me
home,
or homeless, soon, will be.

unrelated

brothers are FORGED
in muscle and blood..
          coined in some COMBAT
  midst folly and mud

growing up OLDER
or younger the spud..
          where flies before GALE
  if forward of scud

chewing the FAT
'til chowing on cud..
          when louder the WHISPER
  far softer the thud

who is the WISER
which more the stud..
          our hero and WINNER
  is swimming through flood

will lead as they FOLLOW
'tween savior and dud..
          and if you are BLESSED
  your brother's a bud

wannabe

New York City of my teens..
    Catholic High School, urban dreams.

A family sharing hand-me-downs,
    borrowed clothes with lots of browns.

As rode through Brooklyn daily, twice..
    Pimps and Brothers paradise.

White boy craving velvet blues,
    Soul Train pants and platform shoes.

When after class, a job I got
    as messenger.. and saved a lot.

Puerto Rican, Ghetto, Black..
    was soon a fashion maniac.

Irish, German made me whole,
    but SUPER FLY was in my soul.

Love my roots yet given choice..
    R & B my chosen voice.

http://www.youtube.com/watch?v=jLUYtTegbjg

you know who you are

her bearing bandwidth.. rigid, blunt
    a narrow slice of grit

when choosing tween a pass and punt
    doth tend to kick the shit

boots the metaphoric dung
    across the many fields

trajectory of feces flung
    aiming what she wields

suffers neither fool nor ace
    savors more the jerk

kiss goodbye your saving face
    her patience doesn't work

Pearly Gates

abed

dander spun with feather dusting
    angel wings and wanderlusting

fall upon my knees in prayer
    my eyes wide open, ever staring

once I sought the brightest white
    when fearing heaven's dying light

twice I craved the black within
    a rusted soul and heart of tin

now I rest on softest grays
    for here I'll sleep my later days

loving others, life I've made
    will face my dying unafraid

Ballet

(Marilyn Monroe – 1954)

Not a tutu. Petticoat.
Dress too tight. An antidote.

    Wrap the corset, underskirt,
    sit unzipped like whipped dessert.

Don't you preach of sin and pride,
of God who orders joy denied.

    Who are you to judge my hand.
    Love it all, I now command.

Thou shalt rouse delight within,
denude each other, heart and skin.

    Look inside those eyes. A child.
    Be that fragile. Open. Wild.

"The Ballerina Sitting"

http://www.youtube.com/watch?v=G1km-z3kf3Q

Blessed are the Peacemakers

they with faces
    burning under FLAK

NAMELESS soldiers
    running from attack

not with fear
    not escaping FIRE

FERRY children
    sacrificial pyre

unsung heroes
    ever give a DAMN

MARTYRS whisper
    'lion saving lamb'

broom

stiffened bristles spitting grit
     shifting dunes of dust submit

as truant flakes ascend and float
     whiff of soot to anger throat

: :

pasty rays of pallid sun
     smoky clouds of cinders spun

in leaden colors losing blush
     twilight hangs with stick and brush

: :

worlds adrift upon each trace
     planets poised in sunbeam's grace

would that ours be like this too
     a speck of life from chimney's flue

http://www.youtube.com/watch?v=kG6O4N3wxf8

157

dread

scribing dark on lonely nights, worries me to brood
when clots of crimson, scarlet gore
need paint my heart with
BLACK

but thereupon the page it lies, a death of reek and rot
fills my nose, invades my dreams
is warmth and love I
LACK

: :

bile snaking up my throat, too soon tonight to sleep
opens scars of severed clefts
bleeding 'til I'm
DRY

blood that pools beneath my desk charms my heart to shrink
all shrivelled like a plum to prune
as soul doth MUMMI-
FY

: :

rhymes that writhe, rhythms foul drive my quill to scratch
ink that burns with wicked whispers
bids me deaf and
BLIND

if any good upon this earth, if anyone is fair
heaven's but a place I fear
a hellish state of
MIND

trample he, ye seraphim, I'm weary of this war
brandish sword and pierce the throat
of serpent writing
VERSE

grant my plume one simple ode, I pray to God for voice
of love and light and those who dare
to slay this author's
CURSE

empathetical

had a knack for sadness ears
could see it in her eyes

like magnets power iron gears
when listening unwise

for there she'd sit and drink you in
allowing woe to drain

silent hands and steadfast grin
receiving of your pain

: :

words she tendered eased the smart
misery is cured

proffered hug endowed with heart
your happiness assured

left alone when door is shut
and you are bounding free

ate within by biled gut
bleeding ears and she

from the Counter

As if the fault were mine,
      the toppled Root Beer Float..

Turned her head and hid behind
      wavy hair and eyes remote.

: :

"A gentleman would buy
      a lady something sweet.

My lips are parched and ever dry,
      am hot down there in all this heat."

: :

Imagined what she wanted
      was really not dessert..

Her stare was far too warm and haunted,
      femme was more a thirsty flirt.

: :

We left the Greasy Spoon
      as bought a jug of wine.

Drank it neath the crescent moon,
      aback the vacant Five-and-Dime.

: :

It satisfied her want,
        all wet and wined and ploughed..

Keenly sated débutante,
        was much obliged and grateful loud.

: :

She sipped the last few drops
        and supped some more from me.

Zipped my fly and fixed her top
        when charged her normal fountain fee.

introvert

(angels back and forth)

hither looks demand of thee
with sleepy eyes, half-closed

worth the trip, a furtive plea
my silent words composed

fold me up and wrap my soul
aquiver in your hand

whisper me the love you hold
as fragile as a lamb

fear the worst, O please be kind
to ever-trembling heart

blithely bothered, undefined
your reaching lips, apart

promise in that potent stare
will pray you understand

know the risk and still I dare
when beg you, *hold my hand*

made in his image

I've not a lot to say to God
who knows the thoughts I bleed

when serpent savors Aaron's rod
with faggot spilling seed

: :

He judges what He gifted me
as making little sense

a covenant His words decree
am left with no defense

: :

joyless nights when still I pray
an answer rips my soul

burn the one who lives as gay
will drown the broken foal

MODERN DANCE

Cryptic, serving critic's whim
      with cutting edge and ANGLED LIMB.

Tutu-less, our retinue
      is enigmatic, novel — NEW.

Starkly clad in veil or less
      as very vexing, I CONFESS.

Can't abide a ballet classic
      — dinosaurs from AGE JURASSIC.

Let me have my avant-garde,
      feet un-slippered, BODIES HARD.

Gender-fluid flesh exposed,
      all nonconforming — THUMBING NOSE.

never alone

Floating on
    familiar ocean,
boat upon
    an old emotion.

Wind has died,
    adrift, alone.
Slack the tide
    and wallow-prone.

Just ahead
    on starboard bow,
soul who fled
    the same somehow.

There, asea,
    our verses waving.
You and me
    as poets, saving.

# of motorsport

Chassis sprayed with ebon velvet
strode across the room.

Dress was short as
legs sped on.

Thought of STP.

            : :

Needing tune-up, prayed
I'd think of some-
thing clever,
awed.

"You.. uh.. look.. umm.."

all I jawed.

            : :

"Lotta mileage on
them plugs,"

heckled back at me...

            : :

Red, my face.
It drew her near,

blazing my ungoggled eyes,
couldn't hear the grandstand jeers.

Hazard flag....

whorled around me, warm
her nitrous licks..

inspecting close this
wreck.

Doubtful I
could win a race.

                         : :

The questioned settled,
silent, spun..

          she revved and headed for the bar.

Dress plunged down a
slender back,

introduced me to
that edge..

the *other* tender, heady cleavage...

miles away
from

Road & Track.

                         : :

Lord, the thought of NASCAR
racing filled my mind
again.

A most delicious oval sought as lost direction,
sense of time..

steering, stirring thoughts aroused,
driving up and down
her strip.

: :

She crashed through crowd,
I dared believe..

returned from pit stop, impish grin and
glasses filled with...

was it wine or gasoline
to goad me on,

fuel my

laps..

PUPPET

(Michael McQuary)

W – ondrous brows of PERILOUS arc
I – mpervious gaze neath shadowy DARK
T – opped with SWIRL, a life of its own
H – elix striped with SERPENTINE cone..

L – ips that beg for more than GLOSS
I – ced with PAINT and candy floss
P – alest powder whitens SKIN
S – inewed TORSO mirrors twin..
T – ake me with you, MARIONETTE
I – 'll hold your STRINGS in silhouette..
C – ommand your heart, lead you in DANCE
K – iss your LIPS..

Why fight romance?

http://www.youtube.com/playlist?list=FLl8HqrfJTK_u-_0skvQ17lg

170

sirens

snuff the scheming, screaming angels
finely drawn, divinely damned

stab me with their steely stalkings
sharpened.. shrilling, thrilling thrust

strip their pointed petals pricking
sticking hearts and picking souls

spark of lumen, seraph searing
glimmers simmer... fearing wings

: :

stay the hallowed, sallowed beauty
born, no torn.. from womb and seed

sip their dripping, drooping dewdrops
curse the days of sweet malaise

screech the banshee, pale the pallid
flowers fling... impaling spring

silent nights of soundless drilling
blood and letting, swilling stink

subtle

(enters diner growling)

Nothing was contained about her mien.. all keen and clear and over-the-top. *Imply* and *infer* simply meant wielding a one size smaller metaphorical hammer.

Should a photog ask a foot be nudged the teensiest bit forward, it was likely placed in an adjoining state.

Bearing, comportment more graceful than most northern elk, was better described as a countenance of bricks in flight... No fine-spun poser she.

Semblance faint is a word duet I'd not be apt to employ.

A girl of extraordinary innuendo and fragile artifice. These compliments paid by no one, ever.. not a spore of prudence in her poise...

..as if drawn in the frailest of pastel tints on a canvas of still molten lava.

: :

And yet, her beauty was inescapable. An ineludibly delicious crumpet... served on paper plate.

Mind you, a very sturdy, lovely and florid Martha Stewart paper plate.. heaped, as well, with gobs of cholesterol-laden mayonnaised salads.

Her Walmart delights spread thick upon a black and white shantung silk picnic blanket... somewhere nigh to Paris, Texas.

Come hithering with her smoky eyes and holey fishnet hose, could attract the attention of hordes of flannelled men in six truck-stops simultaneously.. miles apart... both sides of the Mississippi.

"What's a girl gotta do
         to get a cuppa joe?"

Model breathless reading Cosmo.. angel with her wings yet clipped.. cigarette butts found neath stilettos...

I loved her lack of *savoir-vivre*.

:: ::

"Here, my sweet.." I tendered, pouring...

                    "Tell me when," I begged.

swim

the schooner scarcely left the pier
    when first ker-plunk was heard

bracelet gilded, lustrous bevels, see-sawed
    idly toward its grave

reflecting brilliant tangos 'pon
    the scales of fish like mirrored balls

who oohed and aahed and ached with awe
    around her slipping, silver charms

harbingers, these halibuts
    of other drownings soon to drop..

teased hair

It ain't like I been usin' long...

Still wear tops without no sleeves.   Track marks barely show.

You like my hair?   Bouffed it up for Johnny, meetin' later, playin' pool..

Well, me I'll smoke and powder things...   prolly chalk his stick.

: :

Chalk his stick sounds funny, *right?*

Johnny hustles marks when gets all drunk and spits and kisses hard....

..hard.   *I said that?*

Blouse, I'll open extra buttons just for him..   *but yeah... when late....*   as might be gettin' hot.

Good to keep your lipstick near..   in your pocket.   Reapply when zip him up.

You like that fabric?   Pencil skirt...

: :

And what you need erased?

Like, slit up side and makes me walk all sorta squeezy.... *tight.*
If hard to take it off, is all.

But better than those flares and dizzy circle skirts those
squares still wear.

    Tho easy access there, *ya know?*

: :

I wanna hear a tune,
jukebox fulla doo-wop shit.

    Ahh.. Frankie Ford's a dreamboat... *"Sea Cruise".*

Gotta nickel?

Dance with me.

Mmmm.... I like that.
Hey, you use?

    I'm gettin' kinda itchy, *huh?*

: :

Whaa.. don't get all crazy, baby.

Didn't mean to bother..
only askin' for some extra...   *maybe.*

    Lipstick's in my pocket. I can reapply at anytime.

http://www.youtube.com/watch?v=vakPyR-5ZV0

Time Enough

thought the end
    would never come
        releasing her from pain

but came it did
    and saved her from
        ignoring said in vain

: :

unreserved
    where truth wills out
        she never fought her death

as honestly
    believed throughout
        and ever held her breath

: :

listened not
    to Doctor's plea
        no taking pills prescribed

smiled a
    smile of destiny
        her God was on her side

: :

ache and anguish
    joined the fight
        to test her theory's pith

spread like fire
    through her nights
        as left her creed a myth

: :

sent from high
    above the blue
        a messenger with wings

I plied her with
    a future new
        where seraphs sweetly sing

: :

thereupon
    that final day
        the morning spent with me

unfolded napkin
    swiveled tray
        'but time enough for tea..'

Warm Hands

(Autumn 2013)

Late Saturday afternoon, a father and son took an unfamiliar route on their way to market. Dad was intrigued by the Arts and Crafts style bungalows that defined the streets of their beachfront community, often wandering down unexplored blocks, seeking the unseen.

Indeed, passing one such architectural beauty was their luck today. Not far behind, I stopped as they did.. observing.

It was a view marred only by the huge, menacing, teeth-baring Mastiff on watch behind its fence. Dad chose to ignore the thunderous snaps, snarls and growls, continuing his lesson from a safe distance.. walking and pointing out the tell-tale Arts and Crafts windows, roof details and porch stylings.

The boy heard little of it. Father turned with a gasp, seeing his son kneeling in front of the wrought iron gate, addressing the demonic pooch. The son mumbled soothing words of comfort and reassurance to the yapping, gnashing fangs foaming inches from his face..

It seemed only seconds before the dog sat down.

His bravado waning, his booming, obstreperous barking ere long replaced by a curious, tilted head. He stared searchingly, silently at this wee bit of smiling boy gazing back with sweet and loving eyes.

∷

Father rushed to the scene just as his son reached through the fence, outstretched palm, for his new friend to smell or..

The father's fear appeared unwarranted.

With teeth now hidden behind relaxed lips, the pup's tongue was on a mission, communicating devotion to a boy he only just met. His tail wagging even whilst sitting.

They both arose. The dog continued to groom our child, soon working on his grin.. triggering giggles, smiles and sniggers.. and funny, icky faces.

Dad quickly wiped the sweat off his brow, the hint of wet from eyes and cheeks.. gently brushing dust and slaver off his son's corduroys, offering a scarf for the boy's bathed face.

This *all* felt kind of normal.. for this father, son.

: :

Behind them once more, now in the market's check-out line, heard the shaver ask his dad, "Can you carry the ice cream, please?"

Father agreed with wrinkled brow as the boy volunteered his logic..

"The puppy looked cold. I want my hands to be warm in case I'm lucky to pet him again."

Slipping fingers into hoodie pockets, he smiled at his dad.. who wondered what he did in Life

to find himself so blessed.

You meet 2 people..

One has led a sheltered life. Home-schooled, god-fearing, tempted, seems, by little.

Threat of hell keeps them on the straight and narrow, while prayerful discipline makes up for the rest. Kind and content by all outward appearances, these are good folk.

: :

The other one has sown his oats. Seduced by much as gave in plenty.

Finally getting, grasping, holding that *sex, drugs and rock & roll* don't account for much.. they choose to live more chastely, if purely.. simply because

it just feels better.

But will cherish their memories. Treasure the reckless days and nights.

: :

They are indistinguishable, now, neighbors on the same street.

Who do you respect more?

Who would throw the better parties?

Who might make the bolder artist, actor, author, *dad?*

Who, perhaps, the greater friend?

Tender Years

24 Hour Fitness

I go to a fabulous gym. I have to describe it as such because..
well.. it is in West Hollywood and every member, to a one, is,
quite unrepentantly, fabulous.

I wear old sweats and long sleeves and a baseball cap, so that I
can blend into the more humble walls. No nipple-bearing,
Abercrombie & Fitch, cut-off tanks for me. I can't compete
(anymore) with the bevies of youthful beauties that strut
about the locker room.. or found draped across the racks of
weights.

Yesterday seemed a hint different. Yes, the house music was
blaring. Yes, the buff trainers were posing. Yes, the guys and
gals were milling about, wondering what they'd wear that
evening to show off their freshly hewn physiques.

And yet..

While silently ticking off the last few god-awful reps on an
equally hateful ab-crunching machine, my concentration was
interrupted by a rather vociferously strident voice.. booming
down from 12 to 1.

Then giggling.

Honestly, I was a trifle annoyed anyone would dare disturb my
meditative, i.e. Zen and sweaty, workout reverie.

: :

After a second, similar malfeasance, I glanced right, spotting a
tall and lanky 20-something fella resting between sets. His
mentor friend was commending him on his form, how proud

he was of his burgeoning brawn. The younger man looked pleased and puffed. He was standing more like a little boy might with toes pointing ever-so-slightly inward, bright-eyed face you'd see on a child.. and big, awkward smile inspiring all around him to, unwittingly, grin as wide.

Yes, there was something unusual (some would say 'special') about him. He looked like nobody in the gym that day. This loud, beaming man/child had held onto what most of us lose when we, finally, imagine ourselves altogether grown.

: :

Now, hearing him joyfully, resoundingly count through his reps sounded like music. Felt blessed to be near this beautiful spirit and the pal who guided him on his trek. I tried to think of the right thing to say.. to explain how completely this tiny moment had changed me. How a normal, ab-and-arm Tuesday was tendered by a smile.

But I didn't want to put a spotlight on what they were doing.. on who they were and who they weren't..

and how they made us feel.

: :

I managed to catch the trainer's gaze while working my arms on the next machine. I smiled what I hoped was a *you and your buddy are glorious souls and I am honored to witness such grace* kind of grin...

a lot of words to try and say with misty eyes, silent lips and set of burning biceps.

bike

I've ridden, seems,
a long, long
WAY..

A metaphor
for LIFE
today.

Fields of GOLD,
skies of
blue..

Seeking what,
I PRAY, be
true.

RAYS above
illume the
night..

Bounce off MOON,
reflective
light.

EXERCISE my
right to
ride..

STURDY FRAME
and starry
eyed.

DESERT PRAYER

Teach me well of Eden's ways,
      blazing sun through crystal haze.

Early rise to beat the heat
      if early dinner, sleep, repeat.

: :

New again, I hazard life,
      a never-ending, two-edged knife.

Work is hard 'til heart is fed
      as dreams are easy, cot for bed.

: :

Precious time on tameless ranch,
      pray to God for second chance.

Give me strength as keep me fit
      for midnight verse and daylight grit.

Drafty

(hospital apparel)

no one lives a life of ease
      cutest puppies harbor fleas

with carrots yummy, often peas
      sprinkled pepper kindles sneeze

: :

those that look for guarantees
      who strive for bliss, these wannabes

seeking truth like Socrates
      are often brought to humble knees

: :

see the forest for the trees
      travel far, avoid disease

partake of wine and nibble cheese
      in backless gowns, enjoy the breeze

for kiss

symmetry of eye and cheek
aquiline his nose
jaw of ancient, marbled Greek
likewise, too few clothes

lips of youth that rest apart
for readied breath and speech
or may I dream, betray my heart
for kiss...   an overreach

reverie of age is all
ignore this fevered wraith
too, was handsome, young and tall
am now of little faith

no

hitherto and future-leaning
I will hold my own
know the man whose time is keening
will not turn to stone

and if inclined and toward-tilted
lips will find their goal
as invited, not be guilted
old ones giveth

soul

Hustle

(1976)

I was high school Valedictorian (with all the nerd ideology the word still implies). Summer after graduation stretched into Fall and Winter.

Discovered Disco and John. He taught me to dance.. et alia.

He was Little John to my taller Big John. Though, if you noticed how his trousers clung, *little* was not an apt description.

Met him at a local club, he was living in his car.. an old, gold Cadillac beat up like him.

:::

I'd sneak him down our basement on the coldest nights, after all had gone to sleep, and set him up under a rollaway bed.... with blankets and pillows, and begged him not to snore.

My Mom would come down mornings, put on a wash, later remark how funny the basement smells of late.. like cigarettes and alcohol. I feigned bewilderment.

I remember that scent, can still give me chills.

:::

We (mostly me and my meager savings) found him an apartment, moved him in with all the thrift shop furniture we (me) could afford.

I'd stay overnight when he got too stoned to put himself to bed (often). I'd tuck him in and lay down next, bed no bigger than a cot. I wouldn't dare sleep... not to miss one moment of his warmth, breath, breadth.

He'd jump in the shower with me most mornings, save time getting ready for work (him) and college (me). I tried my best to hide my *approval* as we'd wash each other's backs.

::

I'd often skip classes to spend the day running with him and his messenger job. We'd search the city for addresses, bolting through concrete towers, jumping turnstiles to save on fares, pizza for lunch, paper-bagged beers, and end the day sleeping on each other's shoulders.. taking the J train home.

I still smell the heat coming out from neath the ancient, wicker subway seats. Still feel his manspread knee touching my own.

::

Pizza some more, and then we'd go dancing.

Looking for girls. Praying we didn't find any (me). Hoping to go home

together, alone, again.

idiot savant

(true)

humbled when allied with those
    who've rightly earned their place

whose eloquence in verse and prose
    inspires truth and grace

: :

a mere savant, if learned one
    like seal or monkey trained

an idiot who's just begun
    with words I've entertained

: :

and like a child wunderkind
    stirring, still I lack

the life and time, the seasoned mind
    my banquet but a snack

: :

to those who scribe of lofty things
    who view me as their friend

blest am I to kiss your rings
    and read the words you've penned

learn to

Have you seen or heard of this,
    the thing that some define as — *KISS?*

Beg you, please, reveal to me
    as whether need a law degree?

Is it common wholly two
    or more — or maybe me and you?

I wonder could you show me how,
    if lips would reach should teach me now?

MASONRY

(of bard)

In amongst the open cracks,
    spaces NEATH and tween the stacks,

lies the FORCE that governs truss,
    tensile strength upholding us.

Not the STONE supporting brick,
    grout that joins the layers thick,

NOR the carve that shapes the wall
    but THAT which breathes betwixt it all.

Building blocks composed of you,
    NOTHING that requires glue,

and 'nothing' is another word
    for SOUL unseen but ever heard.

no NyQuil

       like other nights 'twas black the sky
all gainst a moonlit blue

       a fog of frost, the furthest cry
from Spring and blossom's dew

       in midst of Winter, height of chill
with freezing winds and ice

       am poised to tell a story, spill
a fable I've heard twice

                  : :

       there lived an Angel, little one
his feet as big as boats

       who caught a cold, his nose didst run
forgot to wear his coat

       and neither boots nor halo hat
our baby boy, no clue

       as never checked the thermostat
his cold wouldst turn to flu

                  : :

       was nary taught of etiquette
with sniffles snuffed too loud

       to wipe his nose and daub the wet
the proper use of clouds

and here is where the tale grows strange
this cosmic myth of yore

that very night the Heavens changed
from only Moon... to more

: :

our cherub caught a sneezing fit
the nose he wouldn't blow

was spewing Stars like gleaming spit
for Angel snot doth glow

and there they stuck, a miracle
ethereal ah-choos

celestial skies now lyrical
as sticking there like glue

Old Friends

People come into your life for a reason, a season or a lifetime.
— anon

Know this plain about me, please,
as this is how I'm built.

If you are a friend or ex or someone from my youth,
if you haven't heard from me in all these many years,
if you sent me Christmas cards and texts unanswered,

friend requests ignored —

and seemingly I'm deaf or dead
(am more than likely lost).

Be assured you never leave my thoughts, my heart,
that moment fore we fall asleep.

Am one of those who feels the same, no time has passed,
like was is now and then, the present —
I am simply here, again.

Even after weeks and months and years of since we spoke —

This is how I look at life. Like waking
from a dream —

is you.

http://www.youtube.com/watch?v=JMia4Cv8UwA

Outta Date

Hope you drive a TRUCK
someday,
Plymouth, Dodge or
CHEVROLET.

Beat up badly, WEARY
red,
RUSTED chassis, worn-out
tread.

:   :

Years since gears were pushing
THIRD.
Long ago a BEAUT,
I've heard.

Now, might beg some SPIT
and shine.
Pile o' JUNK, the bottom
line.

:   :

Let it run the OPEN
road.
One more race round TRACK
it's owed.

If you peek BENEATH
the hood,
motor's TUNED as rumbles
good.

MAYBE all it needs
is gas,
quart of OIL, squeegee
glass.

Something keeps you TURNING
key.
Something makes you
think of ME.

PED-O-PHILIC

(clothing ad)

'Where is my LIGHT?
Will shadows be
kind
to my SKIN..

      hope I look THIN.'

See that they're YOUNG
with innocent eyes.
Not about
sex, they're KIDS..

      their thinking FORBIDS.

Insecure TEENS.. shape of
a jaw, line of a cheek,
pouting
their LIPS..

      pray for small HIPS.

'Dermis and PORES,
make them
look
TINY..

      don't let me be SHINY.'

Lovely young VIXEN
and maybe the
boys
pretendingly TRUE..

       are drawn to her NEW.

Be drawn to the GIRL
hardly of age,
but
under a SPELL..

       of naked boy SMELL.

'God.. help me MODEL!
Allow this to be my
viral
CAREER..

       starting right HERE.'

Naked, too YOUNG,
tempted to,
too,
is too much to TAKE..

       that image is FAKE.

They think about FRIENDS
as later will chill,
and talk
of the SHOOT..

       the sexy is MOOT.

poised

(Carmen Dell'Orefice)

sharpened angles dare reveal
discerning curves beneath, conceal

rapt and wrapped in trend and time
expressive, lightsome, silent mime

model, muse, and mannequin
seems hardly ever breathing in

ageless style, painted guise
as peering out of yearless eyes

POWER MEMORIAL

(Lincoln Center cross the street)

Looking up past asphalt park
    at so much brick, a building's bark.

West Side Story setting splayed,
    my first day High School. Boy afraid.

Fourteen years on different earth
    when out from subway, second birth.

Suburban raised, now city view
    as turned the corner, walked toward new.

September day, a child survives.
    In four more years, a man arrives.

Ball and books and marching band..
    was taught not read.. but understand.

http://www.facebook.com/photo/?fbid=10159927152554763

Skates

(at the beach)

Disco beauties boogie down,
    roller derby best around.

Pepsi, Pizza, sunny day,
      tube sox, short shorts.. skate ballet.

Solid footing toe and heels,
    8 per pair is plenty wheels.

Plenty skin as plenty tan,
      boom box blasting *'Macho Man'.*

Take a break with sweaty grin,
    boardwalk babes who glide and spin.

Groovin' to the latest beat,
      can't stop dancing whilst they eat.

Small

Was pretty TALL in my youth..
could bump my head ten
   times a day. And ALWAYS last
in lines queued up by height.

   Never thought I'd FIT this box,
nor any box so tight in sod.
   Thought I'd RISE above and
float on clouds.. not sleep in

   DIRT.

                        : :

   Feels SHORT, the span of time
that pressed my Life into a
   tiny mire. LITTLE bits of Johnny
Wolf.. fodder for the worms.

   And yet, my eyes ENJOY the
black. They do not struggle
   open NOW. Dreams are richer,
something I found lacking..

   when ALIVE.

Sneakers

(classic high tops)

Something 'bout the canvas woven
    WRAPPED AROUND your sweaty feet.

      Never new for very long,
        playing Hoops in SUMMER HEAT.

LITTLE IN THE way of arch,
    slackened ankle, cushion nil.

      Yet they rule when serving Court,
        all laced-up and DRESSED TO KILL.

Retro from the day conceived,
    CONVERSE ALL STARS branded first.

      Like 'em when they're worn and weary,
        primo when they're AT THEIR WORST.

Turntable

round and round the vinyl rings
        needle grooves, a singer sings

scratches add percussive licks
        spinning over pops and clicks

DJ mixes interlace
        throbbing quavers quiver bass

12" singles synthesized
        beat and volume canonized

seamless sequence, treble screams
        seamless sequins, fashion dreams

Disco, Soul, Funk and Dance
        reliving youth when given chance

http://www.youtube.com/watch?v=5Ocq8UlLuuw

YMCA

(McBurney Y on 23rd)

cross the street
    from where I sack

an open-windowed
    RUNNING TRACK

mornings waken
    little glee

gaze from bed at
    WHERE I'LL BE

hot as hell
    this August day

as New York City
    SLOWS TO SWAY

enter through
    the vaulted doors

crawling up the
    SAME 4 FLOORS

changing room
    with lockers tall

sipping coffee
    TRYING STALL

so, this is where I prose
my soul.. FREE VERSE freedom rings

soaring flights
in SOARING temps

gym floor fringed with windows high
baking painted cinder blocks.. melting walls.. no A/C

fans the size of INDUSTRY

little more than
swirled as whorled their
HUMID eddies/HUMAN Eddies

fever dreams.. too hot (some were)

heating up
the steamy room
with TWISTING mists of
thicker warmth, thicker arms

of stifling

   NOISY

      GAY-familiar

         things I want possess

how I ACHED for nother's torso
(have or have as mine)

young man prays to LOOK LIKE (be with)

Superman

(or actor playing)
SOMEONE LOVED BY (sleeps with) all

never happened
maybe DID
and

I forgot

back to rhyming
perfect timing

STAIRS FOR CLIMBING

up to track as soggy follows forward, back
cool and dry, in specie, lack

WALKMAN
SOUNDTRACK

something 'bout a Summer gym
as wets and whets when working limb

whiff of pits be ripe and grim.. all in SERVICE

KEEPING SLIM

in SWEAT and SEX and SELF I swim

Writing

asked why I write of homo things

I write of all duets

no thought for whom the singers be..

tenors tuxed or divas gowned

or one of each..

or three

bland

why write if no one reads
or pen when few find words to chew

delicious meals that
sit attracting
bugs

'then write for YOU and no one else'

except if you, the one who
quills, is also just
a picnic
ant

with Summer gone and blanket bare

and so I seem pen less and less
as more and more my
taste for words

unripes

Crampons

There are musical chords that, when part of a progression, can feel dissonant, jarring, incomplete.

At the very least, they create a certain instability that craves harmonic resolution.

: :

I am (finally) done culling and editing some very early pieces. I've never proofed and emended for such a sustained and prolonged length of time. I kept thinking about that musical theory outlined above.

There are parts of a verse (at least my own) that travel through uncomfortable, forced moments.. tending toward disquiet.

The reader begins to doubt what all this throat-gravel means.

(Almost) to a one, I insist my poems resolve at the end. Not entirely unlike The Beatles' A DAY IN THE LIFE. Link to said song below.

The whirling orchestra seems to lose control, climbing to precipitous heights. No one is wearing cleats.

Reaching the summit in splendor.

: :

These things are baked into a lot of poetry.

And sometimes the mountains are hills and dunes.

And sometimes there's no resolution.

On purpose.

We bards drop you.

: :

At least those poets still left climbing
(not fallen off themselves).

http://www.youtube.com/watch?v=usNsCeOV4GM

don't fuck with my friends

friends I count as those I love
and little must you do

to earn your place and worthy of
the love I feel for you

even those I know not much
might somehow steal my soul

whispered words are same as touch
affect me heart and whole

: :

those who cannot fend off hate
are instant chums to me

with no assist they battle fate
when minus prayer or plea

aways away, I hear their cry
in seconds, I am there

kamikaze (least I try)
to slay the beast, I swear

: :

firstly with my words, I fear
I've not a talent for

battling a buccaneer
but with my voice I roar

crazy are my eyes and threats
my hands in fists as scribe

will move to blows with no regrets
for safety of my tribe

: :

won't do much when in harm's way
defend myself, may not

find it best to just obey
no salvo warning shot

so fuck with me and you'll be safe
a faggot, me inside

but hurt a dog, a friend, or waif
I'LL SLAUGHTER YOU.. with pride

facebook friend

expresses self thru mostly memes

wall is full of others, seems

written well by wily teams

prefer my own un-clever dreams

for now

(writer's tinder)

He blazed the page, all purged and burnt,
set with spark from wooden match

if fed by gasoline.

Incendiary similes that
told the story
well.

: :

Pen was bled of poisoned ink.

    Wraith absolved of sin.

: :

'Til once again the itch within,

that scratched his bone
and broke his heart
as ate his soul,

returned,

   rekindled,

  lit.

graceful teeth

never sure if mad or sane
   or speaking out of turn

readers wonder, *is it pain?*
    regard me with concern

does he write to stir the pot
   to seek the limelight's bath?

begging us believe his rot?
    pray I've earned your wrath

: :

bites I chaw in playful verse
   are often false and true

hard to tell if praise or curse
    and do I point at you

grace and toothpaste polish well
   liberties I take

stories that I choose to tell
    the modesty I fake

: :

words can scar with lovely stripes
　　　　wicked poems please

niceties and pie-hole wipes
　　　　　　　naughty, do I tease

burn your page with acid strokes
　　　　not afraid to bleed

tongue and teeth, unholy jokes
　　　　　　and make them want to read

if you ask me

(another writer told me so)

being precious with your words

using only the fanciest thesaurical offerings
of 'DREAM' and 'DEATH' and 'LOVE'

a buncha crap

don't talk about the big issues
means NOTHING to me

tell me a story as to how they run
afoul of the lives you
describe

how your pen deals with that
VERY SPECIFIC set of
circumstances

is what I want to read

how I learn
how we learn

                          : :

defining theeee INDEFINABLE
(stuff in quotes above)
is dumb

how it impacts
a mouse

is
better

                    : :

my stuff is CRAP like
everyone else's

EXCEPT

I never entertain the notion I know
ANYTHING about LIFE

so I'll write about the sand
as it falls through an
hourglass

NEVER about ALL
the sand or domical bulbs or finely crafted
wood and pewter stand

table that it lives upon
or world that it

inhabits

just the 3 or 4 GRAINS
squeezing thru a
tiny hole

that

split

second

illin'

Shakespeare as a shake and bake

    of eloquence and flair, opaque

is how I came to quill obscure

    and felt I found my perfect cure

lure

risky, writing ill of folks
        rousing Karma's rise

but not addressing all you feel is
        by omission, lies

verse can spin a magic web
        make the hate sound cute

tempt the spider with your tease
        then squish it with your boot

mustang

(a writer's metaphor)

rarely, if ever, leviathan dreams
unruly by choice, be tamed with a word

     lasso the moon and yank

rainbows we squeeze into monochrome fonts
rodeo clowns who wrestle with light

     stuffing the sun in a book

broncos unbroken, galloping pages
buck when you wish them to follow your lead

     dropping the reins is advised

opposite

so oft receive more accolades
for inking something dark

    evil deeds and masquerades
    and sinking Noah's Ark

        : :

fiendish folks with naughty nymphs
desires of the flesh

    blood and gobbets, just a glimpse
    the topics ever fresh

        : :

lovers lost, the awful pain
of loneliness, no doubt

    poison, torture, hero slain
    as cannot write without

        : :

abuse, neglect, the end of days
Revelation's curse

    hate and horror, hellish blaze
    and riding in a hearse

        : :

politics and those who flee
war with all its snuff

    the suffering of you and me
    I may have had enough

           : :

raise me up to lift me high
light the lonely hall

    words that heal, oh promise try
    as brighten up your scrawl

           : :

timid is the golden light
humble is its glow

    pen the good, adjust your sight
    and quill the joy you know

pharmacy

(Schwab's for quills?)

like the one that Lana Turner
graced amidst the
starlets
shy

I think I might be ready for
my close-up and a
piece of
pie

finally discovered by the
finders craving
words to
buy

who serve our writers 7-Up
and burgers rife with
cheese and
chips

where wordsmiths go to pose and
daub their lips between
their milkshake
sips

I beg of you to read my prose
recite my rhymes
and skim my
scripts

procurator

oeuvre mine is of a feather
missed by other books

words arranged that oddly tether
moments rhymed with hooks

: :

yet be published, seeking rep
to agent me.. my saws

proof and print them, bind and prep
and sell them to applause

: :

can proffer me as poetry
that tells a long-form tale

as fables, plots in coterie
or jelly donuts stale

: :

I'm nicer than the most who bid
am humble to a fault

perhaps I winked when wrote that (did)
a group of lies.. gestalt

: :

and yet I finish up my plea
with genuflected soul..

take me, please, on bended knee
be proxy for my goal

scribbler's appeal

ADAM, my man, 'tis good what I write
and buckets of readers and coins will alight

    upon golden venture, our pairing, us two
    publish this author, there's money for you

: :

O HENRY, my friend, take time from your day
to read what I sent you, no further delay

    instruct me, your servant, to add what you will
    flog me and flay me and send me the bill

: :

CARRIERE, if you please, mold me to sate
needs yet unmet no longer should wait

    make me comply to the rules of your game
    together we'll wrangle much treasure and fame

seeking validation

barefaced manner, easy laugh
wide-eyed wonder epitaph

    think of me as one who prays
    for online love with hopeful gaze

as writes with heart and clicks submit
whose grin betrays a fool legit

    no one reads your prose or verse
    so wipe that smile.. *dreams disperse!*

practical protects the soul
expect not *likes*, use self-control

    nary gives a flipping fuck
    what you ink.. you gushing schmuck

shushery

censor me with trollish words
 clever comments, not

to the point, you quill with turds
 your ink replete with snot

: :

and though I wish you only joy
 love from mine to yours

I sense a rather lonely boy
 with large proboscis pores

: :

a mother's son, her basement home
 since 1985

Donkey Konging garden gnome
 who never learnt to drive

: :

phallus-shaped of head and neck
 mac 'n cheese you spew

self-acclaimed computer tech
 will masturbate for you

how you slander those like me
　who try in vain to pen

beg you teach us poetry
　and make our runes more Zen

:　:

without assist, we writers should
　inearth our verse in sod

hearken not afore we're good..
　'til scribe like you, our God

too

like so many of her writer familiars
Ilsa took all her favorite words
and combined them over
and over and over

and over
again..

: :

love and *joy* and *death*
used ever so often in her verse

commixed with *dove* and *cloy* and *breath*
in so many disparate, dissonant ways.. she was
sure no one would
notice

variations quite diverse, considering..

: :

and though some
seemed
nice

lost in all their pleasantries..

they simply were
the same to
me

typewriter

Clicks and taps — ZIP. Return.
Ribbon spool — DING! I yearn

    for the days when keys got stuck.
Made an ERROR, outta luck.

    Something 'bout the roller's WHORL,
keys that POP and carbon's curl.

    Liquid Paper never worked —
LUMPY smears of Wite-Out lurked.

Yet the song, the RHYTHM sticks
in my head — percussive mix.

    NATIVE drumming, Call of WILD,
hunt-and-pecking Poet Child.

unsure

not inspired yet, today

to write upon a page

   and yet these digits seem to move

beneath my wrist with rage

"let us have our daily font

allow your mind go rest

   we will find the words for you

and giveth of our best.."

   so whilst I wonder what for lunch

my fingers, keyboard type

   as I will read the verse some morn

discern the good from hype

Thank you

to my online mentors..

who led me to believe I might be good.

Grateful, too, for the Unsplash photographers..

who make our world infinitely

more lovely.

: :

Johnny Francis Wolf is an Autist — an autistic Artist. Designer, Model, Actor, Writer, and Hustler. Yes. That.

Worth a mention — his Acting obelisk — starring in the ill–famed and fated 2006 indie film, TWO FRONT TEETH. The fact that it is free to watch on YouTube might say an awful lot about its standing with the Academy.

Homeless for the better part of these past 10 years, Johnny surfs friends' couches, shares the offered bed, relies on the kindness of strangers..

paying when can, doing what will, performing odd jobs.

Of late.. Ranch Hand his favorite.

From NY to LA, Taos and Santa Fe, Mojave Desert, Coast of North Carolina, points South and Southeast, back North to PA, hiking the hills, and looking for home —

considers himself blessed.

Update: He and Hemingway.. their shared love for six-toed cats and very different writing styles..

have made a home in Key West.

http://www.youtube.com/watch?v=_HPTfbtDKWU

http://www.facebook.com/wolf.johnny

Coming Soon!

Printed in the USA
CPSIA information can be obtained
at www.ICGtesting.com
LVHW071131211123
764425LV00013B/1500